A La Sale
of
Forgiveness and Reconciliation
for Daily Living

By
Robert Salai Zaw Lwin, D.Min.,
A Myanmar La Salette Missionary

Missionaries of La Salette Corporation
915 Maple Avenue
Hartford, CT 06114-2330, USA
Website: www.lasalette.org

Printed in the United States of America

Fr. Robert Salai Zaw Lwin's original document: was submitted for the degree of Doctor of Ministry at the Catholic University of America in Washington, DC. It has been edited by Fr. Ron Gagne, M.S., for publication for the general public.

Booklet Design and Digital Formatting: Jack Battersby and Fr. Ron Gagne, M.S.

ISBN: 978-1-946956-47-7

About the Author:

Rev. Robert Zaw Lwin, M.S., is a native of Myanmar (Burma). He belongs to the Chin ethnic group who live in the west central lowlands – Magway (west central), Bago (south central coast) and Rakhine (central west coast). His home diocese is Pyay (previously Prome) which was established by the American La Salette Missionaries (1937-1976).

He completed his studies for a Bachelor's Degree in Philosophy (Major) and Psychology (Minor) from the University of La Salette, Santiago City, Isabella, Philippines in 2002. He earned a Baccalaureate in Sacred Theology (S.T.B) from the Loyola School of Theology and a Master of Arts, Major in Pastoral Ministry (M.P.M), from the Ateneo De Manila University, Manila, Philippines in 2009.

Beyond that, he completed his La Salette Seminary formation in the La Salette Province of the Philippines and was ordained to the Priesthood on October 12, 2009.

Before coming to the United States, he served as a Pastor of a parish in the Archdiocese of Mandalay, in central Myanmar. He has served as an Associate Pastor at the Catholic Church of St. Ann, Marietta, Georgia. He graduated with a Doctor of Ministry Degree (D.Min) from the Catholic University of America, Washington, D.C., on May 15, 2021.

He and the growing number of native La Salette Missionaries now serving in Myanmar are truly grateful to the North American La Salettes who courageously established the La Salette ministry of reconciliation in his homeland and do their part to make Mary's message known to all her people.

Dedication

This book is based upon my dissertation requirement submitted for the Doctor of Ministry Degree at the Catholic University of America, in Washington, DC.

It is dedicated to:

- my beloved family who nurtured the seed of faith in me that the La Salettes planted;
- all the La Salette Missionaries who worked for thirty-nine years in Myanmar (Burma) from 1937 to 1976 and present La Salettes both in Myanmar and the United States;
- my past and present teachers of faith and theology for their unwavering moral, spiritual, emotional, and financial support.

Fr. Robert Salai Zaw Lwin, M.S., D.Min.

The North American La Salette Missionaries who founded La Salette in Myanmar and served there from 1937 to 1976

JOSEPH KETTNER

JAMES NOONAN

CHARLES RUKUS

BISHOP THOMAS NEWMAN

BRO. RAPHAEL CHIT HLAIGN

JOHN BLUMM

STEPHEN DRESSELL

CHARLES GENDRON

JOHN B. GOOD

FRANCIS LUCEY

JOHN O'REILLY

LOUIS PERPETE

Preamble

The Scriptures tell us the struggles and successes, wounds and healings, misfortunes and miracles in the family life of God's people. Every family has its own struggles to overcome and victories to celebrate. The most challenging reality they have to face is teaching their children how to build the virtues of forgiveness and reconciliation. Since these virtues are essential components of family relationships, it is necessary to revisit the essence of family life so as to heal the wounds of hurts and pains and rebuild broken relationships.

Forming a Forgiving Family

La Salette Religious gather in Myanmar

Parents definitely are tasked with the responsibility to bring up their children so that they learn to mend broken relationships and build a family where forgiveness and reconciliation reign. Pope St. John Paul II in his encyclical letter, *Centisimus Annus* (1 May, 1991) teaches the importance of family life shaped by parents. Parents play a very crucial role in rearing their children in virtues as it is stated below:

> "The first and fundamental structure for "human ecology" is the family, in which man receives his first formative ideas about

truth and goodness and, learns what it means to love and to be loved, and thus what it actually means to be a person. Here we mean the family founded on marriage, in which the mutual gift of self by husband and wife creates an environment in which children can be born and develop their potentialities, become aware of their dignity and prepare to face their unique and individual destiny." (1)

Parents daily interactions with their spouses and their children instill both virtues and vices in their children. Parents must be careful to create a home where God is loved so that their children will be loved as God's children. What parents must teach their children is well stated in the Catechism of the Catholic Church:

> "Parents must regard their children as children of God and respect them as human persons. Showing themselves obedient to the will of the Father in Heaven, they educate their children to fulfill God's law" (CCC 2222).

Since we will be talking about the message of forgiveness and reconciliation given by the Blessed Virgin Mary during her apparition at La Salette, France, it is good to have a quick peek into the stand of the Church on the reality of Marian apparitions. God speaks through events in history to let His people know that He is present in their lives and interested in their daily human affairs. The Congregation for the Doctrine of Faith has to say the following:

> "Throughout history there have been supernatural apparitions and signs which go to the heart of human events and which, to the surprise of believers and non-believers alike, play their part in the unfolding of history. These manifestations can never contradict the content of faith and must therefore have their focus in the core of Christ's proclamation: The Father's love which leads men and women to conversion and bestows the grace required to abandon oneself to him with filial devotion." (2)

The Blessed Virgin Mary gave the message of forgiveness and reconciliation to Maximin Giraud and Melanie Calvat during her apparition at La Salette on September 19, 1846. Maximin was just eleven years old, and Melanie was fifteen years of age. Both of them came from poor families and were uneducated. Although both of them were the natives of Corps, they didn't know each other until they met and realized that they were from the same place. Something great happened while tending their respective herd of cows in the afternoon of September 19, 1846. The Blessed Mother appeared and gave them the message of forgiveness and reconciliation **(3)**

The significance of the message of forgiveness and reconciliation given by the Blessed Virgin May at La Salette on September 19, 1846 is reechoed by Pope St. John XXIII (1881-1963) in his message to the La Salette Missionaries on the apparition's centenary celebration:

"We work a lot for peace, we talk a lot in Paris these days, but there will never be a pacification between human beings without their reconciliation with God and this cannot be achieved without prayer and penance, so the centenary message of La Salette is more than ever a pressing reality... True civilization is found in Christianity and true peace in the prayer, the Our Father, which teaches us to forgive one another, to reconcile ourselves with God and with our brothers (and sisters)."

Pope St. John Paul II in his message to the La Salette Missionaries on the occasion of the 150th anniversary of the apparition revitalized the indispensability of the message of forgiveness and reconciliation in these words,

"May the proclamation of this hope always be at the heart of your encounter with the men and women of today! Through it our contemporaries can be assured that divisions are not irreparable and that it is always possible to repent of one's infidelities, in order to build a reconciled humanity and to follow the Lord, for nothing is beyond God's reach." **(4)**

We hope that this book will help Catholic parents live forgiveness and reconciliation to the fullest in the light of La Salette Spirituality in their daily relationships. Eventually, they shall become models of these virtues for their children and everyone in their family.

General Introduction

In this book, we will explore together how forgiveness and reconciliation can be explicitly experienced and exercised in daily relationships. Drawing from La Salette Spirituality, we will focus on the role of Catholic parents who are the first and most influential persons in the lives of their children regarding the experience and exercise of forgiveness and reconciliation. Catholic parents themselves are also the main proponents and practitioners of forgiveness and reconciliation.

As we embark on an exploration of La Salette Spirituality and its aspects of forgiveness and reconciliation, we appreciate the central importance of the evangelical values of prayer, penance and zeal contained in the message of Our Lady of La Salette. We verify that the importance of these three evangelical values has been consistently referred to in our original *La Salette Rule of Life* from 1858 and onwards.

It has also been referred to in the Official Decree of Approval of our new *La Salette Rule*, given on June 6, 1985, by the Vatican Prefect of the Congregation for Religious and for Secular Institutes, namely, stating that:

- "The Missionaries of Our Lady of La Salette... have as their purpose to be devoted servants of Christ and of the mystery of reconciliation, in the light of the Apparition of Our Lady of La Salette...
- "May fidelity to the message of Our Lady of La Salette inspire the members to live the profoundly evangelical value of prayer, penance and zeal so that, by the witness of their lives [words and deeds], the hearts of [many] may be opened to the Good News which it is their mission to make known to all." **(1)**
- In our study of these values and connecting them directly to Fr. Silvain-Marie Giraud, M.S. (1830-1885) and his work, *The Book of the Spiritual Exercises of Our Lady of La Salette,* **(2)** we will suggest their practical use by parents in their duty to educate and inspire their children in the ways of forgiveness and reconciliation. We hope this

book will be a help in this area of Catholic family life.

Parents as Central to the Life and Faith of their Family

Parents are motivational agents for the unfolding dynamism of pardoning and reconciliation in the lives of their children. Their exemplary life has great impact on their children and provides the most effective lessons for their youngsters. Such accompaniment in the way of forgiving and reconciling is the most visible sign of God's mercy and forgiveness in daily relationships, especially in a case of alienation caused by broken relationships.

Forgiveness and reconciliation happen in the events of daily living. The celebration of the Sacrament of Reconciliation strengthens daily living and the practice of these two conciliatory virtues. Furthermore, forgiveness and reconciliation can strengthen a holistic approach to spirituality if they are rooted and present in every daily encounter with God.

As a La Salette Missionary called to make known the message of forgiveness and reconciliation, this book explores and offers the means and methods that can equip Catholic parents in their co-ministerial duties of forgiving and reconciling. A general understanding of the Pastoral Theology of forgiveness and reconciliation in light of the message of Our Lady of La Salette and its spirituality can help Catholic parents appreciate the significance and applicability of forgiveness and reconciliation to their personal and familial relationships.

Part One presents forgiveness and reconciliation from biblical and theological perspectives. It also explores the relationship between parents employing the teachings of the Church and the ideas and views of theologians and biblical scholars.

Part Two focuses on La Salette spirituality expressed by Sylvain-Marie Giraud based on the message of Mary who appeared at La Salette, France. Sylvain-Marie Giraud joined the first La Salette Missionaries who took care of pilgrims at La Salette on November 13, 1858. It explores Giraud's approach to purgative, illuminative and unitive ways of Christian spirituality as well as the three pillars of La Salette spirituality – prayer, penance and zeal – to help Catholic parents practice forgiveness and reconciliation in their personal and familial relationships daily.

This book encourages Catholic parents to become true ministers of forgiveness and reconciliation in their personal and familial relationships by practicing the three pillars of La Salette Spirituality and Giraud's approach to the Purgative, Illuminative and Unitive Ways of Christian spirituality. They are called by God to become role models that their children can trust and imitate in these critical areas.

Setting the Scene – A Glossary of Terms

As a general introduction to some basic ideas expressed in this book, we provide a glossary of terms which can set the scene for your reflection.

A reconciler is the one who applies the message of La Salette in concrete situations and reminds people that [forgiveness and] reconciliation apply to all. This type of person also initiates and shares "reconciliation [which] is the grace of God." Just as God initiates these two virtues and the apparition itself is the initiative of the Blessed Mother, a reconciler takes initiative to bring them both into daily life. **(1)**

Forgiveness is "an action directed to the removal or annulment of some obstacle or barrier to reconciliation." It is "a stage antecedent to reconciliation" and makes "reconciliation possible" **(2)** "We forgive the wrong-doer when, by the action of love, we repair the broken fellowship and reestablish it upon strong and enduring foundations." **(3)**

"**Forgiveness** begins at home because it is a special kind of love that asks us to remain open, vulnerable, and caring even though we have been wounded, offended, hurt, or pained." **(4)** "Forgiveness is one of the thorniest parts of the reconciliation process." Therefore, it has to have both 'divine and human' aspects, i.e., an 'act of love' and an 'act of freedom' respectively. **(5)**

La Salette spirituality is a spirituality that "has the Blessed Mother's message of God's forgiveness and reconciliation as its foundation for reconciliation with self and others in daily relationships and works... through prayer... penance... and zeal..." **(6)**

Penance means "to look at suffering through the eyes of faith, which teaches us that pain and all life's trials serve to atone for our sins in this life and are the seed of glory for the life to come." Besides, "it means to suffer for others, for their conversion, to appease [the Blessed Mother's] Son's anger, to spare sinners the eternal pain of hell." **(7)**

Prayer is "an elevation of our soul to God in which we request the graces we need; give God thanks for the graces we have received and pay God homage." It is a simple and doable act [of adoration, contrition and thanksgiving] that benefits us. **(8)**

"**Reconciliation** is the work of God, who initiates and completes in us reconciliation through Christ." **(9)** It is "the work and the gift of God...that we [have to] understand how they interact with the work of God and how they become instruments of God's work in all of this." Only then, "the restoration of healing of a damaged humanity" will occur. **(10)**

Sin is "a rebellion against God, contempt for the divine majesty, it is insult and mockery." Every sin reflects the sin committed by the fallen angels upon their refusal to serve God (Jeremiah 2:20). Since their first rebellion against God in Heaven (2 Peter 2:4), the fallen angels still revolt against God using God's own people. **(11)**

"**The relationship of the human person with God** is seen, quite properly, as inseparable from the ordinary problems of living everyday life." **(12)** How to maintain this relationship with God and restore it when it is broken depends on our cooperation with God's grace.

Zeal is "perseverance in penance, of utter detachment from creatures and of union with Mary." It is making her message, "the spiritual sustenance," known to all with the help of God's grace. **(13)** Giraud, 167, 169)

Contents

Part One:

Discovering the Foundations of Christian Forgiveness and Reconciliation

Introduction

In this first part, we present the historical, biblical and theological developments of the Church's understanding of forgiveness and reconciliation.

- In our *first chapter* we will discuss how the Church's understanding and practice of forgiveness and reconciliation historically developed.
- In the *second chapter* we explore the theological foundations of forgiveness and reconciliation.
- The *third chapter* presents the biblical roots of forgiveness and reconciliation utilizing the various views of several biblical scholars.
- In the *fourth chapter*, we put forward the theological underpinnings of forgiveness and reconciliation from the teachings of the Church and its recent leaders.

Chapter One:
Forgiveness and Reconciliation in the Early Church

The Catechism of the Catholic Church provides historical development of the Church's consciousness of the need to forgive oneself and others and reconcile with God. It gives us a glimpse of what it really takes to practice these spiritual attributes. Although staunch Catholics across the globe avail themselves of the Sacrament of Reconciliation on a weekly or monthly basis, the majority of practicing Catholics do it once a year.

Generally, we all are required to receive the Sacrament of Reconciliation before the reception of Communion during the Easter Season if we are in serious sin. (*The Catechism of the Catholic Church hereafter will be referred to as the CCC*) Similarly, the second precept of the Church mandates that "Catholics shall confess their sins at least once a year" to ensure a proper preparation for the Eucharist and to continue "baptism's works of conversion and forgiveness." (CCC, 2042)

The evolution of the practice of the sacrament of reconciliation by the faithful is fascinating. The Catechism of the Catholic Church states:

> "During the first centuries the reconciliation of Christians who had committed particularly grave sins after their Baptism (for

example, idolatry, murder, or adultery) was tied to a very rigorous discipline, according to which penitents had to do public penance for their sins, often for years, before receiving reconciliation. To this order of penitents, one was only rarely admitted, and in certain regions only once in a lifetime to the Eucharist." (1447)

Living as a Christian Minority in a Secular Environment

James Dallen argues that with demographic changes in the Christian communities of the first two centuries came changes in disciplines and lifestyles of Christians. Being a minority in pagan environments necessitated the community to be a loving and forgiving community in accordance with the mandates of the Gospel. To foster unity among members as one family of faith was their main concern and ultimate goal.

Nevertheless, many members fell prey to sins of returning to their former pagan and or Jewish way of life. In order to bring back those who had gone astray, the Christian community demanded change of behavior and lifestyle from sinners. Only then, were sinners forgiven both by God and members and consequently reconciled to the community and God. For instance, Clement of Rome appealed to sinners to repent and ask for forgiveness from God through prayer so as to reconcile with the Church and God. Clement also taught the social dimension of "sin, forgiveness and reconciliation" in light of building an internally cohesive Christian community. (1)

Dallen contends that Ignatius of Antioch counseled every Christian to abstain from sins, while St. Polycarp called for reconciliation of sinners with God and the community to promote and maintain unity. Furthermore, one of the earliest Church writings "a Syrian document from the late first or early second century, the Didache" required sinners to publicly confess their sins in the Church. With this document the exchange of peace came to signify forgiveness and reconciliation, although the document indicates no "formal and ritual discipline in dealing with sinners." The Didache noted:

"On the Lord's own day, assemble in common to break bread and offer thanks; but confess your sins, so that your sacrifice may be pure. However, no one quarreling with his brother may join your meeting until they are reconciled; your sacrifice must not be defiled" (Didache 14:1-2). **(2)**

"The Shepherd of Hermas, an apocalyptic Roman work, further suggested that communal prayer be said for the forgiveness and reconciliation of lax Christians. Especially the Church elders have the responsibility to offer prayers for repentant sinners. The repentant must be welcomed back into the community. Only in the later part of the second century, Irenaeus of Lyon became the foremost teacher of faith emphasizing the need for "conversion to the Church as a factor for receiving forgiveness." **(3)**

Annual Confession of Sins Becomes the Norm

Frans Jozef van Beeck argues why annual confession became a norm in the Church. It was, he contends, only because "the general presumption of sinful habits among the faithful at large had become so strong that the Fourth Lateran Council of 1215 laid down annual confession and communion in the Easter season as the minimum to be observed by all." **(4)**

To highlight the Patristic understanding of forgiveness and reconciliation, Monica Hellwig contends that forgiveness and reconciliation can be received and exercised in daily life. She cited Augustine who recommended praying the Our Father so as to be forgiven by and reconciled with God in an ordinary way. She said that Tertullian suggested sinners do daily penitential acts. The penitents can wear "sackcloth and ashes" as well as fast and abstain to express remorse for their sins. They can also groan and weep in the presence of church leaders and the believing community as a sign of request for their prayers. **(5)**

Marty Slaughter presents how the Church's understanding of God's justice and mercy changed into a legal system between the eleventh and thirteenth centuries. During these times, Catholics were taught by their leaders to see God in a purely human perspective to the extent that God would be pleased only if they do certain things just like doing things for the emperors. Then, it still depends on God either to forgive or not to forgive his people for their sins.

This is so ingrained in the minds and hearts of the people that they were bound to do any penance imposed upon them with a contrite heart, verbal confession and acts of charity. They tend to believe that only heavy acts of remorsefulness bring about forgiveness and help restore relationships. With the evolution of practices of penance given to penitents, the confessor has the freedom to do so in accordance with the gravity of sin. The lightest acts of repentance that can be done easily has been three Hail Mary's. **(6)**

The need for penance and praying the Our Father and the Hail Mary as such are also indicated in La Salette spirituality as we will see in chapter two. The understanding of forgiveness and reconciliation and practicing them daily can lead to a proper and more perfect reception of God's mercy and love. Early Christian communities tried to practice this as they were inspired by God's Word and guided by their leaders.

For your reflection:

Scripture: Romans 12: 11-13,15-17a,18 (*Paul urgings about mutual love*)

Do not grow slack in zeal, be fervent in spirit, serve the Lord. Rejoice in hope, endure in affliction, persevere in prayer. Contribute to the needs of the holy ones, exercise hospitality... Rejoice with those who rejoice, weep with those who weep. Have the same regard for one another; do not be haughty but associate with the lowly; do not be wise in your own estimation. Do not repay anyone evil for evil... If possible, on your part, live at peace with all.

Reflection Questions:
- What good advice about your life do you hear in this reading from St. Paul?
- Which ones of Paul's suggestions have you done recently?
- Whom do you know who has done some of Paul's list?
- Other comments.....

Prayer:
Mary, Constant Example of faith, sometimes we do fail in our responsibilities to love others as your Son loves us. Support us by your prayers that we may remain true to our baptismal call to be more like your Son every day. We ask this through your intercession and in the grace of your Son who lives with the Father and the Holy Spirit, God, for ever and ever. **Amen.**

La Salette Invocation:
Our Lady of La Salette, Reconciler of Sinners, pray without ceasing for us who have recourse to you.

Chapter Two:
Theological Foundations of Forgiveness and Reconciliation

There are various Church documents that can help illustrate forgiveness and reconciliation within the context of my research. It will not be an exhaustive study of the Church's teachings on these subjects. However, I hope and believe that it is a thorough look into the stand of the Church on these areas of faith. First and foremost, why do we need to have reference to the teachings of the Church? One of the reasons why we have to understand and be guided by the teachings of the Church is that Jesus gave the authority to His Apostles to guide and lead the Church. The Catechism of the Catholic Church, teaches:

> "'The task of giving an authentic interpretation of the Word of God, whether in its written form or in the form of Tradition, has been entrusted to the living teaching office of the Church alone. Its authority in this matter is exercised in the name of Jesus Christ.' This means that the task of interpretation has been entrusted to the bishops in communion with the successor of Peter, the Bishop of Rome." (85)

Any loose or partial interpretation could mislead God's people. It is very interesting to learn the way the deposit of faith is interpreted and passed on to every generation. How the Church exercises her authority is explained well in the following statement:

> "Sacred Tradition and Sacred Scripture, then, are bound closely together, and communicate one with the other. For both of them,

flowing out from the same divine well-spring, come together in some fashion to form one thing, and move towards the same goal. Each of them makes present and fruitful in the Church the mystery of Christ, who promised to remain with his own "always, to the close of the age." (CCC, 80, see Dei Verbum, No. 9)

It is essential to know the role of parents in the family before knowing and understanding the teaching of the Church on forgiveness and reconciliation because we apply only what we know and understand in our lives. I would like for the readers to immerse themselves with me into the teachings of the Church on everything we shall discuss in this chapter. We shall have a better comprehension of the role of parents in the exercise of forgiveness and reconciliation in the daily practice of La Salette Spirituality, which we shall discuss in Chapter Six.

What is the Role of Parents?

Before going into forgiveness and reconciliation per se, it would be helpful to look briefly into what the Church teaches on the role of the family and parents in developing relationship dynamics and instilling in their children faith values that Jesus himself teaches. What did Jesus really bring into the world? The Constitution on Sacred Liturgy, *Sacrosanctum Concilium*, powerfully states God sent Jesus Christ into the world as the healer of repentant hearts and the mediator between his children and himself so that in Him "the perfect achievement of our reconciliation came forth, and the fullness of divine worship was given to us." (1)

How do we pass this gift on to others? Parents have the responsibility to convey it to their children. The Catechism of the Catholic Church teaches the role of parents in passing on the teachings of Jesus to their children in concrete daily relationships. They create "*a home* where tenderness, forgiveness, respect, fidelity, and disinterested service are the rule." They must also learn to "acknowledge their own failings to their children" to be able to "better guide and correct them." (CCC, 2223)

The Dogmatic Constitution on the Church, *Lumen Gentium*, states that parents have the duty and responsibility to teach their children and help them grow in the faith. Parents as first teachers of the faith are called to be role models for their children in everything the Church teaches. **(2)** By living out their Catholic faith in secular affairs, parents participate in making God's forgiveness and reconciliation in Jesus Christ known to others. Parents are the lights and guides for their children in the pursuit and practice of forgiveness and reconciliation in Christ in the ordinary affairs of daily life. To highlight the important role of the faithful, some of whom are parents, Lumen Gentium, states:

> "They live in the world, in each and every one of the world's occupations and callings and in the ordinary circumstances of social and family life which, as it were, form the context of their existence. There they are called by God to contribute to the sanctification of the world from within, like leaven, in the spirit to the Gospel, by fulfilling their own particular duties." **(3)**

Pope St. John Paul II on Forgiveness

Parents' exemplary life definitely has great impact in the lives of their children. The teaching of St. John Paul II in his Apostolic Exhortation, *Familiaris Consortio*, #58, specifically speaks of the significance of mutual forgiveness between couples. Their living examples both prepare and sustain the core values of Christian faith that is the imitation of Christ. That is what all baptized promise at baptism and can be fulfilled only with the help of God's grace.

The grace of God can be attained through both personal effort and God's redeeming grace in the daily chores of personal and familial life. This grace is gradually attained and has to be continually sustained. Therefore, gradual transformation and growth of relationship with God and others in the family requires both human and divine participation.

As life can often be challenging, parents, however, have to remember that they are never alone but with the Church in their faith and familial journey. The Pastoral Constitution, *Gaudium et Spes*, states that the Church does know and share the struggles of every individual and their family. She tries to guide both her children and everyone in the society. She knows that humans long and search for meaning in life amidst concerns and fears due to the complexity of life.

They know that the preciseness of modern sciences can fascinate but never give real meaning to life. This radical change in means of communication touches the core of the human person, affects the family, and society at large. Scientific developments, if divorced from God, in many ways hamper relationships. **(4)**

Certainly, for the faithful nothing is meaningful without any relation to God. *Gaudium et Spes* **(5)** states "often refusing to acknowledge God as his beginning, man has disrupted also the proper relationship to one's own ultimate goal as well as his whole relationship toward himself and others and all created things."

We see how technology has influenced and even controlled human relationships. It has created more isolations, divisions and alienation between people, even within the family. Therefore, forgiveness and reconciliation are always needed for rebuilding family relationships. Who can be our role models in this techno-driven and fast-changing world?

The Church and John Paul II as Our Role Models

The International Theological Commission, in their document, *Memory and Reconciliation: The Church and the Faults of the Past*, highlights the witness of St. John Paul II to forgiveness and reconciliation. St. Pope John Paul II during his papacy was an eye-witness to the reality and necessity of forgiveness in the life of the Church. He admitted that the history of humankind has seen the human weakness of the members of the Church. Being sanctified by Christ and the Holy Spirit, the Church takes the responsibility for the sins of her members, both rejoicing over the good deeds of her members and reprimanding those members who commit sins of hate and division.

Holy Mother Church promotes the continual renewal of the life of her members by acknowledging and accepting their faults and sins. She believes and teaches that asking for forgiveness is the only way to grow in relationship with God. She teaches that all Catholics are required to have recourse to God's forgiveness in order that they may become instruments of forgiveness. She has the courage to take responsibility for the sins of her members and believes that God's grace and goodness are more powerful than sin and evil. For this reason, the leaders of the Church must take the initiative to ask for forgiveness both from God and others. **(6)**

The International Theological Commission also reflects on the significance of forgiveness. It reiterates the stance of St. John Paul II, especially the reason behind the Church's initiative to ask for forgiveness from those whom the Church has hurt for two millennia before she entered the threshold of the third millennium.

The Commission contends that Pope John Paul II's initiative was based on the Church's own experience of God's forgiveness. The reason for asking for forgiveness by the Church is that she as Christ's Body takes upon herself every member's sins through all generations. Only then, the whole Church will be ready for reconciliation with everyone and will be able to move on in the next Millennium. **(7)**

The Commission further emphasizes that the sole reason for asking for forgiveness is to purify past memories that reveal the past sins of the members of the Church. The Church needs forgiveness both from God and others for past and present sins committed by her members to be able to continue her earthly journey.

Since her very life continues as it is shaped by the past, she always needs to have her past sins forgiven and be reconciled with them in order to live a new life in Christ with others. The courage and action to ask for forgiveness reinforces the fact that she is both authentic and credible. In doing so, the Church is ready to avoid similar or further damages and scandals in the future. **(8)**

The Biblical Roots of Asking for Forgiveness

To present Biblical roots of asking for forgiveness on behalf of others, the Commission highlights some significant biblical figures like Moses who asked for God's forgiveness on behalf of his people (Exodus 32:30). God's authority to absolve sins and our need of forgiveness are ever more evident in Jesus. We see how Jesus according to the gospel of John (13:34f; 15:1-11; 17:21-26) requires Christians to exonerate others even beyond what human justice calls for.

Christians ask for forgiveness both from God and others because their life is rooted in and revolves around the love of God that sows mercy and reconciles sinners to Himself. The gospels of Matthew (18:35) and Mark (11:25) demand forgiveness coming from the heart because reconciliation requires a change of heart.

On the other hand, the gospel of Luke (15:21) speaks of both vertical and horizontal dimensions of forgiveness and reconciliation. The change of heart helps forgive and reconcile with self and others for he/she has first received God's forgiveness and reconciliation. How does this change of heart affect relationship dynamics?

Reflecting on the story of the Prodigal Son (or the Merciful Father, Luke 15:11-32), Pope St. John Paul II in his post-synodal Apostolic Exhortation, *Reconciliatio et Paenitentia*, speaks of the reconciliation

God offers to his new family. This offer has a long term, lifetime, and even eternal effect that would make the family live in grace, free from sin and death.

The grace of reconciliation helps the family to live in a harmonious relationship with Him and with one another if only they treasure, foster, live out, and pass it on to all generations. Reconciliation is predominantly "a gift of the heavenly Father," but, for a full reconciliation to occur, one has to recognize and return to the original and essential reconciliation that restores loving relationship with God, the Father. **(9)**

Although the gift of forgiveness has been given by God, how does one really receive it? Does it automatically become part of one's life? Although it is freely given, some could not or would not appreciate it due to human reasons. As nothing is automatic in life, we have to learn from others through relationships. Neither are the people who teach us life lessons and values perfect human beings. They also struggle with their own limitations.

From their mistakes they learn invaluable lessons that remain with them for life. Their experiences become their best teachers to the extent that they hand on what they have acquired to the younger generations. One of these values is the significance and value of forgiveness. Only when we forgive one another, can we move on with a new life: It is an essential piece of reconciliation.

St. John Paul II's life and writings

St. John Paul II whose exemplary life touched the lives of many across cultures teaches in his apostolic exhortation, *Reconciliatio et Paenitentia*, that reconciliation is God's gift for humanity as salvation history reveals it. This history manifests God's reconciling love in the Paschal Mystery of Jesus Christ who brought about and completed reconciliation in the baptized. **(10)** When we speak of forgiving and reconciling, we essentially speak of relationships.

St. John Paul II in his encyclical, *Dives in Misericordia (On the Mercy of God)* cites the relationship patterns that break as well as heal as it is manifested in the story of the Prodigal Son (Luke 15:11-32). The patterns that break are thoughts, decisions and actions of the younger son, which cost the younger son his whole being because he lost everything given to him both by God and his own loved ones. The only way to restore his 'dignity and identity' is to be forgiven and reconciled with himself and his father.

Pope St. John Paul II (1920-2005)

The change in his behavioral patterns begins with the realization of his father's unwavering, merciful and loving attitude towards him. We see how the restoration of broken relationship with his father and his family is totally rooted in the fidelity of the father to his own 'identity and dignity' as a forgiving and reconciling father. The power of the father's forgiveness and reconciliation draws the son back to the original state of being a son of a forgiving father.

The son must realize that he has to admit his brokenness in relationships and ask for clemency. The son also knows that realization of his sins means taking actions for the gradual change of lifestyle so as to be worthy of his father's forgiveness and reconciliation. (11)

Pope John Paul II in *Reconciliatio et Paenitentia* reminds us of two realities. *First*, the Sacred Scriptures attest to the fact that God "reconciles the world to himself and thus brings into being a new family of those who have been reconciled." *Second*, God makes all the baptized agents of this virtue. They must understand that "reconciliation is principally a gift of the heavenly Father" who wills to share his unifying love with everyone. His love and gift are not something abstract but concrete and evident in human history.

Its concreteness is found in Jesus Christ who is the visible proof of God's mercy and love. God's "initiative to reconcile us with him and others takes a concrete form in the mystery of Christ the redeemer, the reconciler and the liberator of man from sin in all its forms." Christ came to save us because we can't save ourselves with our own efforts. **(12)**

John Paul II continues to say that Jesus, the great reconciler, teaches his followers to likewise do the same among themselves before they offer prayer and sacrifice to God. Doing so with others precedes reconciling with God. It is the duty and responsibility of the Church to teach this truth and help her members to eventually achieve its fullness. It is in her nature for the Church to work on this objective through her preaching on the message of reconciliation. She also does it by showing how to do it and providing the resources. **(13)**

My belief is that it is mandatory for all pastoral leaders and spiritual practitioners to spread the message of these twin spiritual attributes. To be more equipped pastorally and more prepared spiritually, we must first be personally reconciled with God and one another before we can share it to others. To fulfill this responsibility, it is helpful to look into what John Paul II teaches. He said that Christians are entrusted with "the task of doing everything possible to witness to reconciliation and to bring it about in the world." **(14)** No Christian can fail to practice the teachings of Jesus on these two points.

Pope Francis in his Bull of Indiction, *Misericordiae Vultus* (The Face of Mercy), reminds us that Christians cannot make excuses for not forgiving and reconciling with others. These two virtues constitute the identity of the children of a God who always forgives and reconciles. These are attested by the parables about the merciful and loving God who is always ready to forgive and reconcile with his faulty children. **(15)**

God's offer of forgiveness and reconciliation through Jesus Christ has to be rediscovered, experienced and exercised daily. St. Pope John

Paul II in his Apostolic Letter, *Novo Millennio Inuente*, #37, reminds us that Christians have to reorient themselves to the seriousness of sin as the world around them has lost the sense of sin.

With the realization of the malice of sin, they may come to rediscover the mystery of Christ that offers redemptive love, especially in the sacrament of penance. It is noteworthy that the destruction sin brings upon God's people can be remedied by the Risen Christ's redemptive grace. This rediscovery of sin, forgiveness and reconciliation can be done at home first by the parents, who are the first teachers of faith.

Pope Francis on the Role of Parents in Forgiveness and Reconciliation

Where do we actually begin this ministry? Pope Francis in his post-synodal Apostolic Exhortation, *Amoris Laetitia (On Love in the Family)* reflects on the role of parents in family spiritual life. He said that simple interactions and good ways of communications between parents are inspiration for children. These simple acts of loving relationships manifest the presence of God's love

Pope Francis greets the crowd of people

because God is with those who love others to the best of their ability.

Loving concern for others, truthfulness, and faithfulness to each other are vivid in loving relationships. They manifest the coexistence of human love and divine love. Different gifts are more eagerly shared among children if everyone, especially every parent, does it out of love after the example of Jesus who always loves us. Then, forgiveness and reconciliation are easier to receive and practice. With these foundations, it becomes easier for all to prevent as well as heal broken relationships in the family. **(16)**

Parents Fostering a Positive Attitude

Pope Francis believes that parents can bring up their children to have a positive attitude towards themselves and others. Parents have to foster a positive attitude toward themselves and one another. Such a mindset makes them more lenient and flexible to adjust and adapt to unpredictable human conditions and life's situations that contribute to mistakes, faults and sins. It helps them to forgive others more readily and easily, too.

Since forgiveness is rooted in an upbeat attitude, fostering positivity helps a great deal in the capacity to exonerate others, and it also points to us a bigger picture of every reality. It shows more potentiality than potency. Being affirmative also leads everyone in the family to a greater desire to forgive others even to the extent that one is willing to give way to the needs of others at the expense of their own. Such an attitude opens everyone's heart to be able to forebear, forgive and reconcile with others.

It reduces tendencies towards and eliminates occasions and situations for discord and disunity. Positivity molds all family members to be able to forgive themselves, too. In effect, they are free from low self-esteem that could conceivably cause a psychological impact that impedes forgiveness. **(17)**

As free people, Francis continues, they are not afraid of interacting with others. They also eventually learn to ask for God's grace to be able to renounce the past and live in the present despite limited human conditions. They also have the power and ability to pardon themselves, and consequently, they relate with others in the same manner they're treated themselves. It is very evident that those who can forgive themselves and others have actually experienced God's mercy because God's kindness brings about forgiveness of self and others in the family. **(18)** We see how relationship dynamics begin at home, and it is in the family where we learn everything for better or worse.

The Role of the Family as the First School of Faith

Therefore, Pope Francis exhorts parents to see the significance of their role in the family. Parents have to take extra care in guiding and teaching children Christian values that last for a lifetime. Otherwise, social media and other means of communication could take over their responsibilities. If that happens, the moral and spiritual lives of children are in real danger. Therefore, parents have every right and responsibility to monitor the devices their children use. They have to teach children to learn and imitate whatever is positive but avoid everything that is destructive both morally and spiritually.

They have to guide children on the path of authentic human freedom. They must teach children daily how to delay inordinate human desires and divert their time and energy to positive, constructive and healthy relationships with others. It is in the ordinariness of daily life that children learn to forego and forget everything that is not meant for them as God's children through the trustworthy guidance of parents. **(19)**

The Federation of the Asian Bishops Conference, in their document, *The Catholic Family in Asia: Domestic Church of the Poor on a Mission of Mercy*, especially number 151, deals with the same reality. The Asian bishops construe that, affected by modernism and post-modernism, Christian individuals and families struggle to sustain the values they have held dear for generations. The conflicts between traditional and technological cultures challenge family relationships. Living in a religiously pluralistic society, they contend, where modernists and post-modernists have much influence in everyone's life is challenging.

Social media, the socio-economic and political spectrum have impacted the inner life of every family. People have preferred individual freedom to communal life although the latter alone generates authentic human freedom. But there are also good and faithful families who, despite their own challenges and limitations, reach out to those in need beginning with their family members. **(20)**

In the same document, the bishops contend that this witness of the family is based upon Jesus' teachings that require all Christians to include people from all walks of life. Jesus' teachings also require forgiving hearts because neither anyone nor any relationship is perfect. As humans, the bishops affirm, we all need forgiveness from others and God. **(21)**

The bishops construe that mutual love, forgiveness, and guidance for one another in the family are the remedy for the degradation and erosion of family values. Furthermore, forgiveness is always needed because of the fragility and flaw of everyone. This daily witness, they conclude, is the best message to those who struggle in family relationships. **(22)** But, why are parents significant in this ministry? In this regard, the Church as a parent teaches us the importance of a role model in relational realities.

Witnessing to the Good News

The Second Vatican Council, Ad Gentes, states that Christ commissions every baptized person to proclaim His Kingdom to every nation. The Council Fathers continue to teach every Christian to remember that their way of life is the most effective witness to Christ.

Witnessing to the Good News by their lives will attract others to God because deeds have more impact in lives than words do. They also have to guide others to the awareness of God's presence and the need for it in their lives. Jesus Himself who probes and guides hearts into all truth will help them. They have to free them from the rule of the evil ones and its accomplices so that all live in the protection and freedom of God. **(23)**

The Council Fathers construe that Christians have to journey with others as authentic "witnesses of Christ" who illumines lives with "His light." As others become enlightened by Christ, they will learn to love God and others as new sons and daughters of God. **(24)** Christians are called and empowered by the Holy Spirit to dedicate their lives in the works of the Gospel for their lifetime. As messengers of Christ, they speak with meekness, humility and patience the truth about the suffering Jesus. They dare to obey Jesus and participate in His mission with joy even in the face of martyrdom because of their constant renewal of relationship with Him. **(25)**

In Conclusion ...

Reconciliation and forgiveness are gifts of God given through Jesus Christ. Both biblical figures and the teachings of the Church remind us that we are able to forgive others because we have experienced the forgiveness of God through Christ, and with it our readiness to reconcile with others.

Jacob offering a dish of lentils to his brother, Esau, for his birthright,
by Jan Vistors (1619-1679)

Furthermore, we are able to do the ministry of forgiveness and reconciliation because of our encounter with Jesus Christ through whom God does so with us. Since the early centuries, Christians have practiced and shared these two gifts of God with others. Their Christian life witnessed that ordinary days and activities are also occasions for us to experience forgiveness and reconciliation with God, others and self.

They teach us that our daily personal and communal prayers hone our skills for the spiritual works of forgiveness and reconciliation.

They in no way deny that the sacraments, particularly the Sacrament of Reconciliation, are the utmost sources of encounter with our loving God.

The Church teaches that Catholic parents can practice the ministry of forgiveness and reconciliation in their daily lives. Having understood and practiced this ministry in their day-to-day life, they will serve as role models for their children.

Their exemplary life will help build their daily relationships on the forgiving and reconciling love of God. They will in effect bring healing to broken relationships. This healing will restore harmony in relationships. They will do this ministry with vigor and zeal to bring about the Kingdom of God where forgiveness and reconciliation thrive.

The Word of God (2 Timothy 3:16) indeed helps the Church understand and teach forgiveness and reconciliation in daily life. The God who sent his Son, Jesus Christ, to forgive and reconcile people to himself prepared many significant figures before the salvific event that happened in and through Christ. Some questions often raised when it comes to forgiveness and reconciliation might be answered by some scholars from a biblical perspective.

For your reflection:

Scripture: 2 Timothy 3:16

"...remain faithful to what you have learned and believed, because you know from whom you learned it, and that from infancy you have known [the] sacred scriptures, which are capable of giving you wisdom for salvation through faith in Christ Jesus. All scripture is inspired by God and is useful for teaching, for refutation, for correction, and for training in righteousness, so that one who belongs to God may be competent, equipped for every good work."

Reflection Questions:
- What good examples of forgiveness or reconciliation have your

received from your family or friends?

• How have you been a good example to your family or friends of forgiveness or reconciliation?

• Other comments.....

Prayer:

Mary, Mother of the Church, during your apparition at La Salette you showed us how to be family. Your tender care for the two young witnesses touched our heart and inspired us to be more responsive to the many needs of our own family. Pray that we may made be good models of your loving care. We ask this through your intercession and the grace of your Son who lives with the Father and the Holy Spirit, God, for ever and ever. **Amen**.

La Salette Invocation:

Our Lady of La Salette, Reconciler of Sinners, pray without ceasing for us who have recourse to you.

Chapter Three:
The Scriptural Viewpoint of Forgiveness and Reconciliation within Relationships

Illustration of Hosea and Gomer from the Bible Historiale, 1372

In this chapter, we present forgiveness and reconciliation through the lens of Sacred Scripture. The God who sent his Son, Jesus Christ (John 3:16), to forgive and reconcile people to himself prepared many significant figures before the salvific event that happened in and through Christ. This is a brief exegetical component of forgiveness and reconciliation. In Chapter Four we will present more in-depth approaches from biblical scholars and theologians.

First, it is good to look into the teaching of the Church on the role of the Word of God in Christian life. Pope Benedict XVI in his post-synodal Apostolic Exhortation, Verbum Domini, teaches:

> "When we consider the basic meaning of the word of God as a reference to the eternal Word of God made flesh, the one Savior and mediator between

> God and humanity, and we listen to this word, we are led by the biblical revelation to see that it is the foundation of all reality."
> **(1)**

The experts in biblical studies can teach us valuable lessons about our faith that is rooted in the Scriptures. The lived experiences of biblical figures show us how active God is in the lives of believers.

The Personal Experiences of Moses and Hosea in Old Testament

Theologian and author, Vincent Taylor, argues that to forgive in the Old Testament understanding (Psalm 51:1-19) means to cover or remove sins. It also means wiping out or blotting out sins from the souls of God's children, for it cancels "sins, transgressions, and iniquities." Therefore, forgiveness has to be understood in the context of the Old Testament cult or ritual sacrifices.

Again according to the Old Testament understanding, the victim has to forgive the offender in order to restore their relationship to the point of enjoying "fellowship" with each other. As such, the teachings of Jesus on forgiveness and the reasons behind it can be fully understood only in the light of the Old Testament teaching. Essentially, both forgiveness and reconciliation are gifts of God. These two gifts theologically developed through centuries in accord with biblical meanings, that is, restoration of fellowship with God. **(2)**

Moses' Experience of God's Forgiveness and Reconciliation

The experience of the repentant in every generation attests to God's unlimited forgiveness. It is God who always initiates the process of forgiving and reconciling with his people as attested by the experiences of Moses and of Hosea in the Old Testament. Some of the images of forgiveness rendered to the people by God in salvation history can be found in the Book of Numbers. These highlight the loving God who is ever ready to forgive those who sin against Him. This loving God is more specifically experienced by Moses himself and the Israelites.

J. Edward Owens claims that God is always faithful and present in the lives of His people as experienced by Moses in the Book of Numbers. This book has the presence of the ever-forgiving God as its central theological theme. Here, God through Moses reminds the Israelites that he always forgives their sins of unfaithfulness committed in their practice of idolatry. In this sense, God's people can always count on God's readiness to forgive their sins and reconcile with Him. (3) Whatever is done to God's people is done to God as well. Knowing their sins, God reminds, warns and chastises them to mend their broken relationships with Him. They are reminded that there is interconnectedness of relationships between God and His people.

Frederick L. Moriarty contends that Moses spoke of God as the God who forgives the Israelites although they have gone astray from Him. It is their own fault, not God that got them into trouble. Nevertheless, this kind God of the Israelites is always ready to forgive their sins and reconcile with them. The relationship between the sinful people of God and their forgiving God indicates the interrelatedness of all family members among themselves in all things and with their God. (4) This kind of relationship always begs the need for restoration of broken relationships through forgiveness and reconciliation.

Hosea's Life as a Witness to Forgiveness and Reconciliation

Some biblical experiences that reveal God's readiness to forgive and reconcile with sinners are shared by the prophet Hosea's personal experience. Hosea's experience tells us that God uses many different ways and means to persuade all of His people to accept His offer of forgiveness and reconciliation.

Deirdre Dempsey parallels the attitude of Hosea towards his unfaithful wife with divine attributes of forgiveness. God through the exemplary life of the prophet Hosea makes Himself known as the loving and forgiving God who is ever ready to forgive the sins of his people. It is God who constantly seeks ways and means to forgive the sins of his people.

God's forgiving love exceeds or reaches beyond betrayal, pain and anger caused by his chosen people. **(5)** But, how does God let us know of His readiness to forgive our sins? God must also know the art of communication that attracts and wins over His people.

Dennis McCarthy contends that God proves His forgiveness through the life of the prophet Hosea who persuaded his estranged wife to go back to him. God's offer of forgiveness through persuasion is more for the good of the offended. The call of God for repentance is to restore unity between God and His people as well as between the people themselves.

Sins alienate God's people from God and others at the expense of people's dignity and identity as God's children. Only forgiveness offered by God restores everything to its original state. Furthermore, faithfulness to God and one another maintains fruitful relationships. **(6)**

McCarthy argues that the message of God through the prophet Hosea (2:18-25) also fleshes out what reconciliation between God and His people brings about. God mediates covenantal relationships with His people in order to restore His people's original dignity. He provides everything they need.

Moses by Michelangelo (1475-1564) in Basilica San Pietro in Vincoli, Rome; photo: Jörg Bittner Unna

If they repent and reconcile with Him, whatever they have lost because of their unfaithfulness to their God shall be given back to them. God will make even the whole of creation function again as it is designed to do.

The reconciliation God offers, then, is both for the healing of every disorder caused by sins and to make everything and everyone whole again. **(7)** Hosea's experience tells us how a forgiving heart eventually helps rebuild relationships. The repentant person experiences the irresistible pull of forgiveness offered by their loved ones. That offer itself is the first step to healing that forgiveness and reconciliation bring about. This also sets the tone for reconciliation that is more evident in the New Testament.

Examples of Forgiveness and Reconciliation in the New Testament

We shall now see the responsibility of every Christian to live out and spread the message of forgiveness and reconciliation as the epistles of John and St. Paul's second letter to the Corinthians attest to it. For St. Paul, God not only takes the initiative to offer the gifts of forgiveness and reconciliation but also entrusts every Christian the responsibility to live the ministry of forgiveness and reconciliation.

Johannine Perspective on Forgiveness and Reconciliation

Bruce Vawter contends that it is every Christian's lifetime responsibility to stay connected to Jesus Christ through reconciling relationships with others in daily life. The Johannine image of vine and branches alludes to the relationship between Christ and his followers because Christ is the source of both life and good works of every Christian.

John's epistle (or letter) being very ecclesial in nature teaches that it is only in Christ and through His community that Christians can have life both here and hereafter. This reciprocal relationship between Jesus and his followers as well as between followers themselves determines not only the sustenance but also the growth of relationships. **(8)**

Sandra Schneiders contends that God, out of love for His people, sent His Son to restore relationships by freeing them from the hands of the evil one who leads them to sin. Their sins alienate them from

God, others, and the whole of creation. Jesus, whose very ministry reveals His identity as the Son of God with the vested power, liberates people from sin and death. Jesus through His death and resurrection took away the sin of the world that breaks relationship between God and His people.

St. John and the cup **by El Greco (1541-1614), Museo del Prado**

Sin, Schneiders noted, is a "condition" that Jesus' disciples have to wrestle with and fight against daily. They will overcome it because the leader of the world (Satan) has been defeated by Jesus. Although both sin and its source have been effaced, God's people must still deal with the consequences of sin. Some of sin's consequences are loss of trust in God's love and fear of God's abandonment. God's people also have to be aware of the devil's mischievous acts that make sinners afraid of their own vulnerability and of a sad end they can't foresee. **(9)**

With the removal of the cause and source of death, the lives of God's children are able to blossom. Nevertheless, the devil who knows the bitterness of defeat still tries to deceive God's children. The devil's deception makes them believe that God tries to interfere with their freedom. But, would the author of freedom not respect the very gift he has given us?

Schneiders contends that God in John's Gospel transmits life, although the devil tempts us to believe that God terminates it. God is a loving God who gives life (John 14:6) to His people by giving His Son as the "gift" first at the time of creation and later even as a human person in Jesus' Incarnation. Jesus, the Son of God, is the culmination of creation and redemption. Jesus is the personified prelude to humanity's attainment of eternal life.

God shares his divine life with us through Jesus Christ who took on himself everything that alienates us from God. John understands that to accept Jesus as the gift of the Father means to believe in Him. God gives His life through Jesus His Son contrary to what the evil one espouses and imposes upon us. God through His Son engenders our life even to the point of endangering his own. Therefore, no enmity has to exist between God and His people. Jesus, the Lamb of God, indeed is the savior of the world and of every human person from the evil one who attempts to sever relationships between God and humans. **(10)**

Schneiders continues to argue that Jesus also proved to us that the three lies the devil tells us are wrong.

- First, Satan lies to us that Jesus, the Son of God, sent by the Father to redeem us isn't true. That's why, Satan through the Jewish leaders of the time tried to convince the world that Jesus isn't the vindication of God's supreme love for us.
- Second, it lied that the elimination of Jesus for His blasphemy is the way to bring about justice. On the contrary, Jesus' being glorified in God at His resurrection is true justice.
- Third, it lied that the judgment to execute Jesus by the world through Pilate and the Jewish leaders is a true adjudication. Conversely, only the judgement that Jesus brought about through His victory over Satan and its structures and projects of sin is the true one. **(11)**

Pauline Perspective on Forgiveness and Reconciliation

Johannine theology of relationship with God and the meaning of reconciliation are further developed in the Pauline letters. Joseph A. Fitzmyer, in his commentary on the letter to the Romans (Romans 5:1-11), argues that Christ gives peace and restores hope in Christians by reconciling them to God. Christ liberates sinners from alienation from God and one another and reunites all of them. God makes friends with sinners like making friends with His enemies.

His presence gives life to Christians. And God always takes the initiative to reconcile us to Himself. The proof of that postulate is Jesus Christ whom He sent to reconcile with us. Therefore, we receive reconciliation through the Paschal Mystery of the Incarnate Son, Jesus Christ. The effects of reconciliation are peace, hope, friendship and life in Christ. **(12)**

God has given Himself completely for our sake – that we may have life to the fullest (John 3:16). How do we cooperate with God in His work for it to be fully effective and accomplished? Both God and humans have their respective roles to play in the works of reconciliation. It does take time, energy and constant effort to actualize the reconciliation God has begun in the lives of His people.

Statue of St. Paul in the Archbasilica of St. John Lateran by Pierre-Étienne Monnot (1657-1733); photo: Jastrow

Antonio Pitta argues that the Pauline theology of reconciliation pinpoints how God accomplished it through Jesus Christ for the salvation of all. Paul refutes Old Testament theology, which dwells solely on human effort to earn reconciliation by praying, doing sacrifices, repentance and conversion to win favor with God. Paul stresses the indispensable role Christ plays in reconciling us to God. Nevertheless, Paul does not deny the need for people to repent and convert.

Paul's point is that it is God who initiates, accompanies and perpetuates reconciliation. People have to gradually and gratefully accept it. Therefore, reconciliation is rooted in and relies on God. It is, however, focused towards and comes to fruition upon human receptivity and response. (13)

It is essential to understand reconciliation's ecclesial dimensions. As the believing community relies on right relationships between God and members as well as between members themselves, it is better to understand reconciliation's ecclesial dimensions.

John J. O'Rourke contends that the Pauline theology of reconciliation has Christ the Crucified as the source and resource. Through his Paschal Mystery sinless though He is, Christ brought about reconciliation for all humans. Nonetheless, people can still lose what is offered to them if they do not practice it in their relationships with others. For this reason, Paul speaks of reconciliation as a practicality that all must live out in their daily interpersonal relationships in order to have effect on everyone's life. What we have received (that is, being reconciled with God) also has to be shared with others. (14)

Pauline theology helps us understand the forgiving God who reconciles with any repentant sinner. Where is his basis for his claim on this forgiving God who always reconciles with his people as being different from the Old Testament? Where and when can one exercise reconciliation?

Joseph Plevnik underscores the triumph of God through and in Christ over sin and death. This victory over sin and death wrought by the suffering, death and resurrection of Jesus Christ is foundational in Paul's theology. It reflects Paul's own conversion experience (Acts 9:1-19) and the Christ-event that is the most manifest in the crucified and resurrected Christ.

Something consistent in Paul's theology is the sonship of Jesus in relation to the Father. Paul's dictum is that we understand God as the forgiver and reconciler only in the context of Jesus' identity as the Son of God. Therefore, the core of Pauline theology is the relationship between the Father and the Son as well as the relationship between His followers and the Father in Him through the Holy Spirit. **(15)**

Mark Gignilliant argues that the Suffering Servant Isaiah speaks of undergoes suffering for the salvation of others. God redeems sinners through the Son who offers forgiveness. Jesus died as a vicarious and representational mediator for the sinners as Paul understood in conjunction with Isaiah 40-55. God through the death of Christ renews things and reconciles the world. Paul presents Christ as a passive victim as prefigured by Isaiah's Suffering Servant.

For Paul reconciliation means having right relationship with God who forgives sins and reconciles us to Himself. Paul equates sins and rebellion of Israel with those of nations of every generation. All of these barriers, Paul construes, are eradicated by Jesus the Suffering Servant. God in this way saves people of all nations. Paul proclaims that God always graciously and freely initiates the actions to forgive sins and reconcile with sinners. **(16)**

Rudolf Bultmann argues that God provides new circumstances and occasions for us to reconcile with Him. God renews our friendship broken by our sins. God's peacemaking with us is to restore right relationship with Him. To reconcile means reversing our relationship that has been diverted by the evil one away from God.

The God who doesn't count our sins that offend Him initiates this process through Christ Jesus. It doesn't depend on any human effort but God's own doing. Humans have to freely receive it as God gives it as a gift.

Reconciliation takes precedence over human endeavor or even of human's awareness. Although the reconciliation God has offered is already accomplished in Jesus Christ, Paul's contention is that men have to respond to it with faith in God. It totally depends on His grace to be able to accept it and live it out. God through reconciliation effaces sins that make God and humans enemies. Paul construes that God in Christ frees His people from the conditions that lead them to sin as well as from the forces of sin that overwhelm and bind them. **(17)**

Reconciliation then is Christo-centric because Christ's life and ministry brought it to completion, and it also connotes the Trinitarian and ecclesial dimension because of its relational spectrum. As God and His works can be understood only in the context of perfect relationship between the Father and the Son and the Holy Spirit, so forgiveness and reconciliation are best understood in the context of right relationship.

Of all relationships, family relationships provide an excellent starting point for the works of forgiveness and reconciliation. The story of the Prodigal Son is indeed the most significant story of forgiveness and reconciliation in the family setting.

Vincent Taylor argues that the story of the Prodigal Son extends and enriches the essence of forgiveness. The story of the Prodigal Son provides developmental stages of how the father restores more rich and humane relationship by forgiving and reconciling with his son. It also makes the Pauline theology of reconciliation clearer by giving it a deeper theological meaning. **(18)** How they are linked to each other is interesting to examine.

Antonio Pitta, in his commentary on the second letter of Paul to the Corinthians (2 Corinthians 5:19-21), highlights Paul's exhortation to all Christians to embrace Christian responsibilities. Paul said that

Christians are entrusted with the works of reconciliation. The prominent figure in the works of reconciliation is Christ Himself who reconciles us to God and to one another. The Pauline understanding of reconciliation references the story of the prodigal son where the father steps out of his way to welcome and reconcile his repentant younger son. The father also tried to convince and invite the older son to participate in the works of reconciliation and live it out.

Paul contends that Christ entrusts Christians with the responsibility to faithfully continue his ministry of reconciliation with the help of God's grace. **(19)** We see here how the victim initiates and includes everyone in the process and perfection of reconciliation. The role of the victim makes reconciliation holistic and encompassing. The question is how parents, like the father in the story of the prodigal son, can concretely experience and exercise forgiveness and reconciliation daily.

Pheme Perkins argues that Paul as an apostle asked the Corinthians through his second letter to them (2 Corinthians 2:5-11) to exercise the ministry of forgiveness, especially by forgiving the person who transgressed against him (here Paul is teaching the Corinthians about the essence of forgiveness by asking them to forgive those who offended their teacher, Paul himself). Living an exemplary life as an apostle, Paul also taught the Corinthians as parents would their children. His letters manifest the essence of being a minster of forgiveness and reconciliation.

Christians, Paul argues, have to be totally different from others who did not follow Jesus. The Corinthians have to see God as the source of these complementary virtues so that they will learn to see them as God's gift and work. Paul urged the people of Corinth to see him from a divine standpoint so as to understand his role as a minister of forgiveness and reconciliation.

His conversion experience of the merciful and loving God in the Risen Christ is the greatest proof of his ministry and the basis for every parent's ministry of forgiveness and reconciliation. **(20)**

The Story of the Prodigal Son illustrates the necessary steps in the process of reconciliation, namely, the prodigal son's realization of the need for forgiveness, his taking actions to ask for it, and having the courage to reconcile with God and others. One might wonder how the prodigal son came to realize and decide to return to his father.

Carroll Stuhlmueller states that the son had the courage to do what everyone who has come to his/her senses would do. The son's remembrance of his father's love that always forgives ignites his desire to return to and reconcile with his father. This story speaks of Jesus' readiness to forgive sins and reconcile with sinners. **(21)**

The Return of the Prodigal Son **by Pompeo Batoni (1708-1787)**

Gerald O'Collins argues that the story of the prodigal son gives us a perfect example of an authentic love that always forgives, reconciles and unites everyone with God and among themselves. Such love fully gives and receives. It finds its perfection when it is reciprocated. Consequently, it safeguards and enhances "the identity and freedom" of the repentant. The story gives us a glimpse of how God joyfully awaits sinners' return for reunion with Him. **(22)** Attitudinal change is very significant here.

Vincent Taylor argues that our understanding of Christ and His ministries determines the essence and depth of our faith in Him. The maturity of our faith in Christ shapes our attitude towards Christ and sin as they both have relational dimensions. Theology of faith and sin develops accordingly as it bespeaks of everyone's relationship or the brokenness of it with God, the Church and others. **(23)**

Taylor underscores the message of the Gospel that we are called to hate sins and long for freedom from them. The Gospel also announces the gift and growth of life in Christ both individually and communally. The Gospel commissions every baptized to share the gift of life with others in the wider society and the whole of creation. Furthermore, the Gospel teaches the continuing work of Christ to meet the needs of men, especially bringing joy both here and hereafter. The Gospel teaches us that the relationship between God and his people through Christ Jesus frees them from the bondage of sins. Their whole being grow in Christ and full redemption is assured in eternity because of their relationship with Christ. **(24)**

We have discussed the teachings of the Church and the understanding of theologians and scholars on how God brings about forgiveness and reconciliation. The Church and scholars attest to the fact that God works through His Son and the people He chooses for the accomplishment of this divine relationship. Our understanding of forgiveness and reconciliation through biblical lenses prepares us to dig deeper into theological meaning of this unique rapport.

Having understood experiences of forgiveness and reconciliation by prominent figures of the Church and of the Scriptures, we are led to dive deeper into the experiences of these virtues by people of our times. The applicability of certain virtues in everyday life is indispensable to inspire and impact the lives of others, especially of parents in the family. In the following section, we shall see practical steps experts use and encourage us to use for the practice of these virtues.

For your reflection:

Scripture: 2 Corinthians 5: 17-21 (*Pauls' gospel of reconciliation*)

So whoever is in Christ is a new creation: the old things have passed away; behold, new things have come. And all this is from God, who has reconciled us to himself through Christ and given us the ministry of reconciliation, namely, God was reconciling the world to himself in Christ, not counting their trespasses against them and entrusting to us the message of reconciliation.

So we are ambassadors for Christ, as if God were appealing through us. We implore you on behalf of Christ, be reconciled to God. For our sake he made him to be sin who did not know sin, so that we might become the righteousness of God in him.

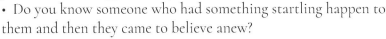

The Conversion of St. Paul on the Way to Damascus, by José Ferraz de Almeida Júnior

Reflection Questions:
- What are three things Paul is saying to you in this passage?
- Recalling how Paul was converted by falling off his horse and becoming blind for a time, before he regained his sight. How would you feel if that happened to you?
- Do you know someone who had something startling happen to them and then they came to believe anew?
- Other comments.....

Prayer:
Mary, Mother of Evangelization, in your visit with the two children at La Salette, you welcomed them and spoke to them about things of faith – prayer, worship, and other habits of faith. Pray for us that we not forget the basics of our faith today and always. We ask this through your intercession and the grace of your Son who lives with the Father and the Holy Spirit, God, for ever and ever. **Amen.**

La Salette Invocation:
Our Lady of La Salette, Reconciler of Sinners, pray without ceasing for us who have recourse to you.

Chapter Four:
Various Scholars' Approaches to
Forgiveness and Reconciliation

Since all relationships experience hardships, quarrels, and misunderstandings, forgiveness is the foundation of reconciliation and likewise, precedes it. Reconciliation restores relationships into their original state. Consequently, it will be hard to move on with life which necessitates relationships. It is every Christian's responsibility to practice reconciliation as commanded by Christ. The only way to better understand these spiritual attributes is to see them through lenses of the Gospel which speaks of Jesus Christ.

The Prophet Isaiah **by Michelangelo (1475-1564),**

Sandra Schneiders' and A Biblical Theology of Forgiveness

In this chapter, we will see some references to the message of the Blessed Mother and the La Salette Spirituality as the theological views of scholars are presented. Linking the various theological perspectives on forgiveness and reconciliation with the main components of Chapter Five, concerning the La Salette Message and Spirituality, can widen our understanding of forgiveness and reconciliation.

Sandra Schneiders contends that Jesus Christ who is the Lamb of God (John 1:29) bequeathed the Holy Spirit to the Apostles (John 20:21-23) so as to build a new community where forgiveness and reconciliation reign. The new community of Jesus will have the life that is totally distinct from the Old Testament rituals of atonement.

That life offered by Jesus through His sacrifice and forgiveness canceled his disciples' sins of "betrayal, denial and abandonment" so that they would share the same with others. "Jesus sacrificial death" is the reversal of "violence in a victory not only over personal fate but over death itself." **(1)**

Schneiders contends that Jesus' sacrifice was for the forgiveness of the sins of God's children so that they can be reconciled with God. Jesus' sacrifice frees His disciples in every generation from offering any sacrifice as a scapegoat. Jesus' last supper and His death on the preparation day before the Passover Feast fittingly symbolize the Suffering Servant and the Sacrificial Lamb to be offered for the sins of all, as it was prophesied by the prophets. Believers have to be instruments of forgiveness and reconciliation for others as they themselves forgive and reconcile with God and others.

We have the freedom to forgive or not to forgive ourselves and others. However, our refusal to forgive others contradicts God's two-fold gift for us. Unforgiveness is the rejection of the sinner and holding on to the sins of the sinner. This indeed runs counter to the essence of our faith in God who always forgives sinners. Unforgiveness heals no one, while forgiveness heals everyone. Unforgiveness often breeds evil intent to retaliate and revenge those who have sinned against us. It indeed disrupts and destroys relationships with others and God. **(2)**

How was Jesus Seen by the Jews as a Bothersome Scapegoat?

Schneiders argues that Jesus was condemned to death as a scapegoat because he belonged to the region of Galilee where political insurgencies against the Roman empire arose. Besides, the people of Galilee were considered despicable by the religious authorities due to their social status. Additionally, for the Jews, Jesus could not be a Jew, but a Samaritan the Jews did not associate with. Or He could probably be an illicit son of Mary. As an unmarried man in His thirties challenging religious institutions cast doubt on His credibility and competency. Furthermore, Jesus spiritually looked weird because He dealt with evil spirits.

His claim of being equal to God in authority and majesty as the Son of God was worse than every strange thing about Him that the Jews did not have. This blasphemous statement was valid enough for Jesus to be executed. Whatever reason they had, scapegoating Him helped civil and religious authorities avert the impending societal disorder. (3) In this light, we will understand why Mary at La Salette reminded us to do penance for others that will be discussed in chapter two.

Was Jesus Isaiah's Suffering Servant?

Schneiders continues to argue that God works through the violence that humans did to Jesus. In Johannine theology, Jesus is the one whom the Suffering Servant of the Old Testament prefigured. Jesus died as the Servant and Son as Isaiah's prophecy of the silent lamb is echoed in Jesus' silence in Pilate's presence. His coming, suffering and death are essentially meant to expiate the sins of His people. God's love and the purpose of Jesus' self-sacrifice take precedence over His violent death.

John vividly presents the voluntary act of love shown by Jesus for His friends. Jesus participated in the life-giving love of the Father by offering His life for them.

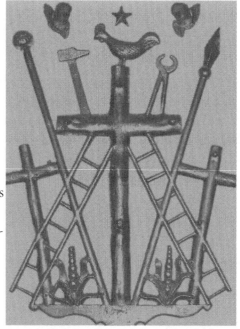

Instruments of the Passion, including the hammer and pincers shown of Mary's La Salette Crucifix; photo: Poussin jean

His freely giving of Himself grants us freedom from sin and death. **(4)**

In Chapter Six we will see why Mary at La Salette spoke of humanity's need for freedom from sin and the weight of people's sin that caused her suffering. We will also understand, as Giraud's method presents, our need for voluntary penance or active penance for others.

Schneiders explains how God the Father accompanied Jesus as He underwent the weight of people's sins. God works through human spite that led to the execution of Jesus and in the Suffering Servant as the Isaiah prophecy vividly states in Isaiah 53. God in Jesus fulfills His divine will, not human will, by freely and willingly accepting suffering and death. God overcame human brutality with non-violence. "By entering into and taking on the role of the scapegoat, He could render it forever impotent by exposing once and for all its satanic mechanism."

Jesus' suffering and death abolished the evil and violent process of scapegoating. Those who, mostly guilty of sins or crimes, undergo life's similar vicissitudes are consoled by Jesus' fate because Jesus, though innocent, could endure the injustice of suffering and death. They find hope in Jesus who freely underwent and bore suffering. Although to scapegoat means to hide the victim's innocence and the perpetrators' guilt, the case of Jesus exposed everything with His resurrection. **(5)**

After His Resurrection, Jesus Forgave His Dispirited Disciples

Schneiders continues to say that Jesus offers forgiveness, not revenge, to everyone who directly or vicariously participated in the act of execution. Through forgiveness, He enabled His disciples to freely accept the love of God freely given to them. The resurrected Christ in His "full glorified humanity" embodies complete "forgiveness" and exhaustive "reconciliation" that encompasses eternal life.

Jesus taught His disciples to do the very exact thing to everyone to whom they preach the Good News. They have to share the gifts of forgiveness and reconciliation with others. For this sole reason he commissioned them to evangelize others to believe in the lamb of God who took away the sin of the world and destroyed the power of evil over God's people forever. **(6)**

Michael Hurley associates the need for forgiveness in human relationships with St. John Paul II. The whole life of St. John Paul II, he argues, witnessed to the necessity and urgency of forgiveness in the life of the Church before the second millennium dawned. St. John Paul II witnessed to forgiveness both in his preaching and practice. He asked for forgiveness for the sins committed by the sons and daughters of the Church against others, especially against fellow Christians, in the past. He on behalf of the Church forgave the sins of others committed against the Church.

In 2000 Pope St. John Paul II
Asked Forgiveness for the Church

His most significant and lasting teaching on forgiveness is well stated in his Apostolic Letter, *Tertio Milennio*, issued in 1994 as the Church prepared herself for the new millennium 2000. His acknowledgement of the sins of the members of the Church and asking for forgiveness from the offended, St. John Paul II believed, would purify the Church so as to be ready for the new millennium. **(7)**

Hurley contends that this bold move of the pope to forgive and ask for forgiveness shows the world that the Church is a

**Pope John Paul II
in Austria in 1988**

56

mother who reaches out to others in order to love them. The pope's exemplary leadership reinforces the Church's ministry of reconciliation. Despite some pushback from some leaders of the Church and the eastern Churches, the pope went ahead and did change the attitude of others towards the Church. The pope showed that mutual forgiveness is essential for both parties to reconcile with each other and mend broken relationships. Restoration of relationships comes only with forgiveness and reconciliation.

Forgiveness, the pope taught, is that which we can grant and ask for. It is both for the rehabilitation and reinstatement of the offender and reestablishment of broken relationships. It is perseverance in loving others so that the offender will repent and atone for his/her sins until the offender and the victims are reconciled. It precedes and is prerequisite for reconciliation. Definitely, both of these virtues need God's grace and time. **(8)** The life and ministry of Jesus Christ whose life holy men and women emulate in every generation witness to forgiveness and reconciliation.

Raymond G. Helmick and Rodney L. Petersen state that the whole corpus of the Gospel contains the message and story of forgiveness. It is the actions of the Trinity as vividly manifested in Jesus' life and his Paschal Mystery. The way Christians understand forgiveness is rooted in the bigger storyline of the Gospel. Essentially, it is entrenched in the workings of the Trinitarian God as made manifest in the Paschal Mystery of Jesus Christ – His life, death, and resurrection. **(9)** We have demonstrated the centrality of forgiveness for the Christian life. How, then, shall we practice forgiveness in daily life?

Doris Donnelly's
Seven Concrete Steps of Practicing Forgiveness

Doris Donnelly argues that to forgive isn't practical or logical or a common attitude for most of us. In reality, forgiveness is a laborious and painstaking endeavor. Even those who have made it their lifestyle would tell us that it is never easy to practice it. But they gradually grow in it as they embrace the reality of life that necessitates forgiveness. To forgive is a continuing venture that needs constant and consistent effort. There are "stages that act as landmarks through the forgiveness process, stages that direct us, eventually, to freedom." **(10)**

Donnelly provides seven steps for forgiveness.

- *The first step* requires us to accept the fact that we are hurt and the pain it causes. This requires honesty and humility to recognize that we are vulnerable to any feeling or action that hurts or harms us. As susceptible as human nature is, it is not necessarily as easy as we think to recover from hurts. It does take time and effort to get over hurts.
- This awareness and admission lead to *the second step* where we make a decision to forgive those who hurt us. This decision is the result of finding meaning in the pain caused by the hurt. This is also a tactic to survive the hurt or endure the aftermath of an incident. It leads us on the correct path.
- *The third step* tells us to recognize that "forgiveness is a process and that it takes time." **(11)**
- *The fourth step* explains that "real forgiveness always, always involves a little death that is definitely not pleasant and easy to endure." It can be likened to the death of martyrs, who always have an attitude for the freedom of the offenders. Louis Bouyer states: "Coming from the Greek word *martys*, which means witness, this term, at least since the Apocalypse of St. John which uses it frequently, has come to designate the principal witness given to Christ by Christians who accept death out of faithfulness to their Savior." **(12)**
- *The fifth step* calls for learning from those who have experienced forgiving their offenders. Their stories can teach us valuable lessons that it is possible to forgive the offenders and forego tendencies and desires to linger around past hurts inflicted upon us.
- *The sixth step* requires us to forgive ourselves because Donnelly contends that "another's forgiveness can be real in our life only if we forgive ourselves." Learning to forgive ourselves is freeing ourselves from the burden of guilt, hurts and pains. Forgiving ourselves means convincing ourselves that sins, mistakes, hurts and pains are

part of life. It also means to approve ourselves, while condemning our past wrong deeds in all its honesty. To forgive ourselves readies us to accept God's forgiveness. Forgiving ourselves is the key to acceptance of the forgiveness of God and of others to be able to live a new life.

• *The seventh and final step* is seeing those who hurt us from a new angle, perspective or new light. "Fear, prejudice, lack of education, isolation, insecurity, unhealed hurts of the past" can hinder us to forgive and free those who have wronged us. As God always forgives us, we must learn to forgive and free others (Matthew 6:14-15, 18:15-35). **(13)** Donnelly believes that "one of the ways we can strengthen the practice of forgiveness is by willing it, by wanting it even if it appears impossible. Maintaining an attitude of forgiveness is a healthy step that prepares the ground for actually forgiving." **(14)**

What does that freedom mean? To what extent is a sinner free from wounds and the stigma of sins? Jesus has the answer for such questions for He endured and overcame all pains and hurts any human would ever experience. Freedom is very crucial in the ministry of forgiveness and reconciliation. If humans can freely accept God's offer of forgiveness and reconciliation, they will have no excuses not to forgive and reconcile with others.

Robert Schreiter's Theology of Reconciliation

After His resurrection, Jesus appeared to His disciples to let them know that their sins are forgiven (John 20:19). Jesus also instructed them to do the same to others who will in many ways sin against them.

Robert Schreiter agrees with the Church on the fact that Jesus conferred upon the apostles the capability to exercise the ministry of forgiveness. The responsibility of forgiveness Jesus entrusted to Christians is indispensable for the restoration of relationship between the offender and the offended. Christians are duty-bound to forgive others although it is very challenging and seems impossible much of the times.

Moreover, Schreiter also argues that forgiving someone of his/her sins appear to look like ignoring and brushing off the reality as if it never happened. It is worse to think of the victim as being punished once again, particularly when the culprit does not even like to admit what he/she did. Schreiter also acknowledges that what it takes to forgive someone is colored and dictated by different cultures. (15) Then, how will forgiveness and reconciliation be preached and practiced?

Schreiter construes that reconciliation is God's work. God both takes the initiative and

**Fr. Robert Schreiter, C.PP.S.,
teacher, lecturer and author**

perpetuates it in and through Jesus Christ who is the reconciler between God and humans. Although God is the initiator, humans have their role in the process of reconciliation. They have to foster their relationship with God because reconciliation happens only with the help of God. (16)

He contends that this indeed is not automatic but takes time and energy to foster and perfect reconciliation. As humans, we are often driven by our instincts. Therefore, we have to guide and tame our impulses. This difficulty should not be a hindrance in learning to forgive ourselves and others.

However, there has to be a way to attain the better way of living our life in Christ who teaches us to forgive and reconcile with ourselves and others. Forgiveness and reconciliation free the sinner so much so that a person shakes off the shackles of the past and freely moves forward to a new future. (17) How to attain the freedom forgiveness brings takes a long and even a lifetime process for some. Therefore, it requires unwavering attention, tireless effort and God's grace.

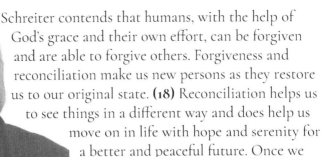

Schreiter contends that humans, with the help of God's grace and their own effort, can be forgiven and are able to forgive others. Forgiveness and reconciliation make us new persons as they restore us to our original state. **(18)** Reconciliation helps us to see things in a different way and does help us move on in life with hope and serenity for a better and peaceful future. Once we have experienced the forgiveness of God and have the ability to forgive others, we are ready to reconcile with others as well as do the ministry of reconciliation.

Fr. William Nordenbrock, C.PP.S., teacher, lecturer and author

William Nordenbrock, in his talk "Ministry of Reconciliation: Methods Rooted in Spirituality," contends that God is the starting point of the works of reconciliation. This divine gift is a directive for us to carry on the mission His Son has launched. It is the continuation of God's work that has its origin in the ministry of Jesus Christ. **(19)**

Similarly, Schreiter contends that Christians believe that God is the prime source of reconciliation. God is also the principal agent because He manifests his works in His own plan for an estranged handiwork. God draws us back to Him and enables us to commune with Him in the salvific work of His Son. **(20)**

Schreiter's Understanding of Forgiveness and Reconciliation

Schreiter offers His understanding of forgiveness and reconciliation. He explains that forgiveness necessitates for the forgiver to see the extent of a wrong act or sin. It encompasses all consequences that affect everyone. Some often take time or even a lifetime to heal and restore relationships. For this reason, Schreiter argues that "human forgiveness" has to be modeled after "divine forgiveness." He distinguishes between these two by saying that divine forgiveness comes from God's love that overcomes every sin. This love of God was at work during the creation, the incarnation, and the Paschal Mystery.

All of these three came into existence because of that love. God continuously offers His love to mend broken relationships, strengthens existing relationships and lets everyone share the communion of His love. Jesus suffered and died to show us the cost of this divine love that always forgives. Divine forgiveness is rooted in this costly love that is voluntarily and abundantly given to all for eternity. God can forgive and always forgives sinners because of His great love for them. **(21)**

How about human forgiveness? How does it work? Schreiter argues that human forgiveness functions differently from divine forgiveness. "Human forgiveness is an act of freedom." It "involves both a process and decision." It is a process because one sets oneself free from the control of the past. To gain this freedom from the past, one has to undergo a kind of purgation. One has to revisit past hurts and admit that painful things happened. Depending on the nature, intensity and enormity of the incident or event, the process will differ.

One has to decide to move on into a differing future with mindfulness and firmness. One has to make "a conscious decision" every day for a new future. **(22)** What could be practical steps to exercise reconciliation? How difficult is it for those who are weak, wounded and therefore live their lives with lots of pitfalls?

Robert Schreiter's Five Elements of Reconciliation

Robert Schreiter argues that the only way to heal human relationships is giving emphasis to "the horizontal dimension of reconciliation." Schreiter provides five elements that could help us to better understand reconciliation in relationships between humans.

- *Firstly*, he is consistent with a theological standpoint regarding reconciliation. God initiates and completes it because it is His mission. God alone comprehends the complexity of reconciliation and how it will work out.

• **Secondly**, God prefers the vulnerable and the rejects of society to start the healing process. This is the fact that both God's prophets and his Son attested to. This in no way acquits the offender but rather assumes that the victimizer shows no repentance. The victim's effort to reconcile and heal the brokenness can also influence the offender to repent.

• **Thirdly**, reconciliation renews the lives of both victim and the offender. It even opens a new horizon that is beyond their imagination.

• **Fourthly**, every painstaking effort and the things they have to go through to heal the victim and broken relationship is "patterned on the passion, death and resurrection of Jesus Christ." Only then, everything that the victim and the offender undergo has its meaning and is less painful.

• **Finally**, complete reconciliation and healing happen only when God restores the "humanity of the victim." **(23) (24)** The victim has to embrace the way of Jesus as his/her spirituality so that he/she will be able to forgive and reconcile with the wrongdoer.

Marian Maskulak argues that the reason behind the difficulty of the victim to forgive his/her offender lies in the victim's inability to distinguish the humanness of the doer from his/her acts. The initiative of the victim to forgive and reconcile with the offender will pave the way for the offender to repent from his sins. **(25)**

William Nordenbrock, in his presentation given to La Salette Missionaries in Orlando, Florida, contends that ministers of reconciliation must see beyond existing challenges and conflicts so as to address covert issues that affect relationships. He openly and eloquently said, "the ministry is not just putting out fire; we also need to help make things fireproof." **(26)**

To be Jesus' faithful ministers of reconciliation, we need to receive the gift of forgiveness and reconciliation. Receiving the gift means that we allow ourselves to be forgiven by and be reconciled with God. Returning the gift means to forgive and reconcile with others.

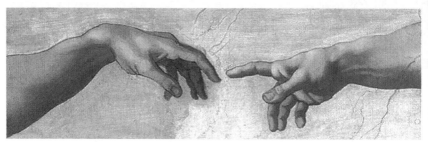

The Creation of Adam, **Sistine Chapel ceiling
by Michelangelo (1475-1564)**

Anthropologically, it must begin with personal life so as to be ready to move up to the higher level, which is a familial reconciliation.

Once the grace of reconciliation is effective in the family, the fragrance of it will surely affect the lives of others, even those who live in very complex situations. It is indeed very challenging to do the ministry of reconciliation to people with different backgrounds, attitudes, sentiments and lifestyles. On the other hand, the grace of God will help overcome hindrances so as to prepare them to enter into the grace of reconciliation.

All human beings reflect God's loving presence because they are created in God's very image (Genesis 1:27). However, the challenge for all is to show equality in the exercise of respect. How far can we show respect for all regardless of age, gender, social status, and religious affiliation? The amount of effort we have exerted to respect one another matters. Whether we are comfortable or not, respect is an initial step for reconciliation.

Monika Hellwig's Theological Viewpoint on Reconciliation

Monika Hellwig argues that God through the Holy Spirit always invites, welcomes and reconciles every sinner to Himself. This very act of God, once accepted and perpetuated by every repentant sinner, gives life to the person and his/her community. To be reconciled with God means to be integrated again after being alienated by sins. Reconciliation gives "meaning, purpose and joy" to everyone. Sins make us lose meaning that only reconciliation can restore. The parable of the prodigal son in the Gospel of Luke (15:11-32) provides a typical image of a lost life caused by sin and regained by reconciliation. Sins alienated the son from himself, others and God. The son did return first to his true self, and then to the Father who welcomed and reconciled him to himself. What sins cut off through unlawful assertion of his independence was reconnected by the loving embrace of the father's reconciliation. **(27)**

Hellwig contends that Jesus' very life and ministry speak of God turning towards sinners. He invites, welcomes and accompanies them in the works of reconciliation. Jesus shows us through the story of the prodigal son that God sees things differently from humans when it comes to sinners. God's forgiveness and reconciliation are offered to all who repent regardless of their sinfulness and duration of their sins. God's forgiving and reconciling love is indiscriminate and offers an everlasting freedom. **(28)**

She contends that God both initiates and perpetuates reconciliation in Jesus Christ. Therefore, Jesus definitely accompanies us in finding our way back to the Father. Jesus reorients us so that we may regain our focus on the right path that leads us to our forgiving God who is ever ready to reconcile with us. The God who loves us knows what it is like to be alienated from His love when we are frustrated, suffering, and losing meaning in life. Jesus through His suffering, death and resurrection offers forgiveness so that whoever accepts it will be reconciled with God. **(29)**

Hellwig construes that Jesus' life, despite being counter-cultural, portrays what we all are created and called to be, that is, God's image and likeness (Genesis 1:27). Jesus shows us the way to live as God's image and likeness in the sense that we have to resist temptations. His struggles against the authorities of His time shed light on existential realities of sin and of human frailty. These are often espoused and executed by human institutions, be it religious or civil. Christians have to make continuing efforts to discern and be open to conversion. They as members of the Church have to spearhead the works of forgiveness and reconciliation. They have to find ways and means to encounter the forgiving and reconciling love of God in their daily life. (30)

God in the ordinaries of life, Hellwig describes, lets us experience His forgiveness and reconciliation in our relationships with others. God's unconditional love that welcomes, forgives and reconciles makes us remember Him and return to His loving embrace in our respective biological families and faith family. We can freely accept God's forgiveness and reconciliation. They are not meritorious but God's free gifts for all who need them. These families can mediate or mitigate the freely given gifts of forgiveness and reconciliation. (31)

Brian P. Flanagan argues from the ecclesial point of view that reconciliation is the act of restored relationship between God and his people as well as among the people themselves. It is what St. John Paul II did with all fellow Christians and people of other faith traditions before the second millennium. The pope showed the world that the Church is aware of its own weaknesses and sins. Only by asking forgiveness from those members of the Church who have offended and by being reconciled with them, the Church will be cleansed of sins of the past and credible enough to pass on the faith to younger generations.

The pope asked for forgiveness on behalf of the whole ecclesial community because the Church journeys as a family unit. We have to admit the sinfulness of the whole ecclesial community. Every member of the community has to regain the consciousness of the social dimension of sin and the effect of forgiveness and reconciliation on every member of the Church. This awareness and practice will help the mission of the Church flourish. (32) This reception and practice of forgiveness and reconciliation help us receive God's gratuitous gift more readily.

Benjamin Brown says that everyone is free to receive God's gift of Himself. Despite our sinfulness, we can have a grateful and willing reception of God's unwavering love given to us without any strings attached. The things that hinder us to embrace God's loving and forgiving presence are our self-reliance, independence, self-delusion, and thinking too highly of ourselves as better than others. Only radical change, although very difficult, will liberate us from the web of repeating the same sins. This change can happen only with the help of God's grace.

Jesus as the visible proof of God communicates Himself to us in history. Jesus teaches us how to evade temptations as well as escape from the bondage of sins that the world put us in. Jesus also teaches us how not to compete with others, not to be blind and prideful. On the contrary, Jesus bore our sins on behalf of others in the non-violent way. God becomes our friend again by giving Jesus as the best gift. *First*, God offers forgiveness for the sins of our ancestors and of our own. *Second*, God enables us to receive His gift of forgiveness without impeding our freedom. God also teaches us the consequences of our sins and our accountability for them so that we may exercise our freedom well and return, even after we sin knowingly or ignorantly, to Him who is ever good and loving. **(33)**

Normand Theroux's Appreciation of the Place of Reconciliation in La Salette Spirituality

If we look at God's invitation to reconciliation with Him, His ways are always persuasive. Even when God reprimands and chastises His people it is always in hope of winning them back to His reconciling love. God persuasively presents the truth about us and Himself. His ways are gentle even as He offers His free gift of reconciliation.

Normand Theroux, M.S., in his book, *The Face of the Reconciler*, contends that reconciliation is a gift from God to be received and shared with others. Return to God by being forgiven and forgiving. This gift is to be exercised by all in the Church through various ministries. As it encompasses every state of life, anyone can live it out. Life's calling may differ but the call for the ministry of reconciliation is equally required in all states of life. **(34)** Theroux continues that "reconciliation is most often applied to individuals in specific situations. Whoever would perform this ministry needs to examine the manner, style and spirit with which Christ Himself exercised it in the gospels." **(35)**

Sharing it in accordance with pastoral needs is the key to the fruitfulness of the ministry of forgiveness and reconciliation. Nevertheless, very few would like to share it with others as spirituality has been privatized. Perhaps, the analogy of donating blood would be appropriate in pinpointing

Fr. Normand Theroux, M.S., scripture scholar, teacher, retreat director and author

the significance of sharing because blood saves lives. Sharing the gift of reconciliation indeed save relationships, which are the life of ever human person.

Only when one has harmony within oneself, is it possible to forgive and reconcile with others. This harmony comes into fruition only when one experiences forgiveness from and reconciliation with God. Both God's grace and human effort are fundamental in our struggle to become who God wants us to be. The destiny of every person, particularly of a believer, is to be in harmonious relationship with everyone. That includes with his/her very self. Why can't one live freely alone and grow without others? Christian life calls for a life that is built upon a holistic relationship, which needs both God and neighbors.

From God we have the gift of forgiveness and reconciliation to be shared with others. The call to live them out is not for a sporadic, seasonal, and conditional but regular, daily, and unconditional spirituality. God through His Incarnate son reconciled the world to Himself and renewed relationship with His people who now live as a new family. This reconciled family of God always has to cleanse themselves of the poison of sin that causes confusion, division, and rift in their lives.

This journey of reconciliation requires much sacrifice. We have to get closer to God who has a great concern for our daily affairs. God alone cures our indifference and remoteness from him and one another. God's offer of the Good News must be welcomed and accepted by all of His children. Those who have been reconciled with God must in turn invite and welcome others so that they will also experience the power of God's reconciling love. Invitational and welcoming atmosphere and loving ambiance scatter fears and strengthen faith in God. Similarly, they help build trust both in God and one another. We have to meet others where they are by showing the power of God's loving presence through our presence. So, what happens to those invited and welcomed?

Theroux contends that the God who abhors sins but loves sinners realigns their lives through reconciliation. They are neither half-awake or half-alive but fully alive and totally committed in their daily relationships with God and others. Everything they do conforms to God's will. They now have regard for both God and others. Sins that affect everyone and infect every aspect of life are cleansed from their lives. Holiness is restored.

Reconciliation straightens out social dimensions of sinfulness as well as holiness. None of these come about without any suffering. Suffering precedes salvation as attested by Christ Jesus Himself. To have the strength to bear sufferings, incessant prayer is indispensable. Such a prayer is important for the ability and attitude to love God and others. **(36)**

Theroux contends that Mary at La Salette emphasized the indispensability of prayer using the threefold extremity of expressions such as abandonment, dutifulness and incessance. Mary prays and we should likewise do so as not to be abandoned by Jesus. It is our duty to pray both for ourselves and others. Nothing should hinder, let alone stop, our desire to pray and for praying at all times. Everything that is said about the importance of prayer is that it connects us with God and others to generate life for all. The only way to survive and thrive in spiritual life is to have life in Christ through prayer. **(37)**

Summarily, then...

In Chapters One and Two, we have discussed a brief history of the practice and development of forgiveness and reconciliation through the centuries. We see how it changed from a spiritual component of early Christians' daily life into a legal system. It was systematized from the individual to the communal practice for the good and certainty of every member's spiritual and faith life.

More specifically, in **Chapter** Three we delved into the biblical aspects of forgiveness and reconciliation using

Our Lady of La Salette **from our Chapel in Angola**

the experiences of Moses and Hosea together with their respective communities in the Old Testament as models. The perspectives of the Johannine epistles, the Gospel of John and the story of the Prodigal Son in the New Testament are used to discuss forgiveness and reconciliation. The Johannine epistles and the Gospel of John highlight the restoration of relationships through forgiveness and reconciliation and the life in Christ for faithful Christians. The story of the Prodigal Son explains the process of forgiveness and reconciliation.

70

We have also discussed the Pauline theology of forgiveness and reconciliation that speaks of Christ as the concrete expression of God's forgiveness and reconciliation and how God in Christ Jesus liberates us from sin. In the light of the works of biblical scholars, we, likewise, discussed the responsibility of every Christian to be instruments of forgiveness and reconciliation.

In **Chapter Four** we saw in our survey other scholars' view on forgiveness and reconciliation with a particular emphasis on Paul's second letters to the Corinthians (2 Corinthians 5:16-21) and Paul's personal conversion experience (Acts 9:1-19) that impacted the lives of others.

Theological foundations of reconciliation are explained within the parameters of *the parents' role in the formation of their children*. Here we use the teachings of the Church to highlight the importance of reconciliation and forgiveness in parents' personal and familial relationships. The lives of the Church and Pope St. John Paul II are used as role models for parents to emulate.

Then we present the works of Sandra Schneiders on Jesus' sacrifice for the forgiveness of sins and reconciliation between God and his children and Doris Donnelly's explanation of the laborious and painstaking nature of forgiveness and the seven steps to attain forgiveness. Included in our discussion was Robert Schreiter's understanding of reconciliation as the work of God and five elements that help attain the new life reconciliation brings about.

Then, we explored Monika Hellwig's explanation of the essence of reconciliation in interpersonal relationships and daily lives. She argues that reconciliation can be experienced and practiced in the concrete events and interactions of a daily living. The ideas of other scholars are used to reinforce the ideas of the aforementioned main authors.

Lastly, we presented the La Salette Missionary Normand Theroux's understanding of how reconciliation is relevant for everyone from all walks of life and applicable to every circumstance and situation of daily living.

The relevance and applicability of forgiveness and reconciliation will be discussed more in detail in **Chapters Five and Six**. There we will also look into the works of Sylvain-Marie Giraud and the three pillars of La Salette Spirituality to understand the implications of our common shared ministry of forgiveness and reconciliation.

For your reflection:

Scripture: John 20:19-23 (*Jesus forgives the sins of the disciples and gives them a ministry of reconciliation*)

> On the evening of that first day of the week, when the doors were locked, where the disciples were, for fear of the Jews, Jesus came and stood in their midst and said to them, "Peace be with you." When he had said this, he showed them his hands and his side. The disciples rejoiced when they saw the Lord. Jesus said to them again, "Peace be with you. As the Father has sent me, so I send you." And when he had said this, he breathed on them and said to them, "Receive the holy Spirit. Whose sins you forgive are forgiven them, and whose sins you retain are retained."

Reflection Questions:
- In John's view of the post-resurrection appearances, Jesus appears to the disciples, forgives and does not mention their sins of unfaithfulness to their Lord during his passion. What qualities are evident in Jesus' act of forgiveness?
- Have you ever met someone who was generously forgiving to you or another? What qualities of faith did they show?
- Other comments...

Prayer:

Mary, Reconciler of Sinners, at La Salette you show us the qualities necessary to be a reconciler. Your gentle manner with the two frightened children calmed them as they stood before you. Your compassionate response to their inability to fully understand your words was refreshing. And your patient presence with Maximin who needed your encouragement to remember the incident with his faither at the field of Coin.

Mother Mary, continue to pray for us that we may learn from your example how to be reconcilers in our needy world. We ask this through your intercession and in the grace of your Son who lives with the Father and the Holy Spirit, God, for ever and ever. **Amen**.

La Salette Invocation:
Our Lady of La Salette, Reconciler of Sinners, pray without ceasing for us who have recourse to you.

Part Two:
Principles for Living Out Christian Forgiveness and Reconciliation

The Palsied Man Let Down through the Roof
by James Tissot (1836–1902)

Chapter Five:
Giraud's Spiritual Exercises as Rooted in the La Salette Message

Introduction

Sunday Offertory Procession during outdoor Mass in Madagascar

We now look into "The Book of the Spiritual Exercises of Our Lady of La Salette," by Fr. Sylvain-Marie Giraud, M.S. (1830-1885), the basics of which can help Catholic parents exercise their own ministry of forgiveness and reconciliation. It is mainly focused on the history of Christian Spirituality and especially on Fr. Giraud's view of the Purgative Way, Illuminative Way and Unitive Way in the light of Mary's message at La Salette.

Here the three pillars of La Salette Spirituality – prayer, penance and zeal – will be incorporated into Fr. Giraud's La Salette Spiritual Exercises. The ideas of other scholars will be used as needed so as to reinforce Fr. Giraud's suggested methods of La Salette Spiritual Practice.

The La Salette Apparition

At the outset, it would be good to look briefly into the history of the Apparition, the Congregation and the life of Sylvain-Marie Giraud. Emile A. Ladouceur, M.S., in his book, *The Vision of La Salette: The Children Speak*, describes how Mary, the Mother of Jesus and our Mother as well, appeared to Maximin and Melanie, young cowherds, on the mountain, in the jurisdiction of La Salette Parish in the Diocese of Grenoble, France on September 19, 1846. She made known the message of God's reconciling love that offers forgiveness and reconciliation and gave them the responsibility to make it known to all God's people. **(1)**

La Salette mosaic emblem in
St. Peter's Church
in Dagenham, England

The Apparition as the Spiritual Foundational Event of the Congregation

The Constitution of the Missionaries of Our Lady of La Salette states that the La Salette Congregation was founded in the light of the Apparition of Mary at La Salette on September 19, 1846. The authenticity of the apparition was officially approved by the bishop of Grenoble, France on September 19, 1851. With the decision to construct a shrine in honor of the Blessed Mother, six diocesan priests of the diocese of Grenoble were chosen to be the first missionaries of Our Lady of La Salette. They were officially entrusted with the responsibility to be ministers of forgiveness and reconciliation as well as accompany pilgrims at the shrine in 1858. **(2)**

The La Salette *Rule of Life* states that, following the example of the first missionaries, the community grew in number and became a

Fr. Sylvain-Marie Giraud, M.S.
(1830-1885) at age 35

Pontifical right in 1890. The community is composed of religious priests and brothers who dedicate their lives to the "ministry of reconciliation." Their evangelical vows and apostolic life reflect the message of Our Lady of La Salette. They have indeed made the message of Our Lady known to everyone they serve. **(3)**

The *Rule of Life* continues to explain that in response to the invitation of Mary to participate in Christ's work of forgiveness and reconciliation, the missionaries have been serving in missions to bring people back to God. They help people obey God's will and strengthen their faith in him so as to overcome temptations and avoid sins. Their apostolic works of forgiveness and reconciliation find their foundation in daily relationships with God and among themselves. **(4)**

To continue this mission more effectively with the faithful of God, Sylvain-Marie Giraud wrote Spiritual Exercises in the light of the message of Our Lady of La Salette.

Sylvain-Marie Giraud – A Holy Man with Unique Gifts

Now, we look briefly into the life of Sylvain Marie Giraud whose work shall be the main focus in this chapter. Giraud was born in a small town of southern France on September 30, 1830. He was ordained a priest for the Archdiocese of Aix-en-Province on December 17, 1853. He served God's people as a Diocesan Priest until his retreat on the mountain of La Salette in August 1857. His time of reflection on the Holy Mountain reinforced his desire to become a religious to

the point of returning to the mountain on September 18 and partic-
ipating in the Eleventh Anniversary Celebration of the Apparition.
He realized that La Salette indeed was "the compass of his life."

After much resistance from both his bishop and fellow clergy, he was
finally allowed to join first La Salette Missionaries on November 13,
1858. As he himself was drawn by the message and the Apparition
of Mary at La Salette, he conducted the Spiritual Exercises for the
pilgrims in three ways such as:

- **First: the Purgative Way** that reflects on the importance of penance as emphasized by the Blessed Mother;
- **Second: the Illuminative Way** that reflects on the light coming
from the cross the Blessed Mother wore
- **Third: the Unitive Way** that focuses on putting Heaven into perspective in daily life.

Fr. Jean Curtet, M.S. (1909-1993), edited and published this work of
Sylvain Marie Giraud in French in 1946 in honor of the 100th Anniversary of the La Salette Apparition. **(5)** Fr. Donald L. Paradis, M.S.
(1932-2015) revised and published this work in English in 2005 **(6)**

Jon Sobrino and the Nature of Sin

To understand the works of Giraud as well as the essence and need of
forgiveness and reconciliation in the following sections, it is necessary to look into the reality of sin as well as its personal and social
dimensions. We will also understand why and how God continuously
turns to us, although we turn away from him every time we commit
sin.

Jon Sobrino, in his book, *Christology at the Crossroads*, argues that
Christ preached about his Kingdom that is always onslaught by
personal and social sins. Jesus' theological view of sin is that it contradicts both God and His Kingdom. Jesus came to eradicate sin because
it assaults the core of human existence and the human heart.

To follow Jesus means to take away everything that enables one to sin. Elimination of sin alone constitutes following Jesus in a radical way. If sin is not eliminated, sin leads people to an eventual rejection of God's Kingdom altogether. The rejection of God's Kingdom forces people to misuse and abuse their self-created power to the extent of oppressing others. **(7)**

Fr. Jon Sobrino, S.J., Spanish theologian, author, teaching in 2013 at University of Central America, Sala de Mártires, El Salvador; photo: Johan Bergström-Allen

John Sobrino construes that sinners personally refuse to receive the coming of God's Kingdom and socially reject to participate in the anticipation of the imminent coming of the Kingdom. Their sins break their relationships with both God and their fellow human beings. Any broken relationship is the product of the abuse of power. Overemphasis on the preference of one's own endeavor to God's and others' leads to the abuse of power. This indeed turns into sin. **(8)**

The fallen angel abused its freewill and power to revolt against God. Consequently, it lost its place in Heaven. This fallen angel together with its company of other fallen angels always tempts God's children to fall into the same pit of perdition (Revelation 12:7-9).

How do we make known to people the message of forgiveness and reconciliation so that they can apply them in their daily lives? These experiences of forgiveness and reconciliation happen in daily lives. Aside from the healing by God and the believing community through the Sacrament of Reconciliation, there is another level of healing that occurs in daily relationships.

- What do forgiveness and reconciliation in daily life mean?
- How did these practices evolve?

• Can one be truly forgiven and reconciled with self, others, and God even when one cannot or does not participate yet in the Sacrament of Reconciliation?

• How crucial is the role of parents for their families in the experience and exercise of forgiveness and reconciliation?

Practical Everyday Parenting and Giraud's La Salette Spiritual Exercises

Catholic parents must be aware of the significance of praying, doing penance and having undying apostolic zeal as part of their daily life. Parenting is not easy but it is part and parcel of being parents to their children. It can be likened to doing daily penance for their children.

Mitch and Kathy Finley contend that parents have the duty to protect and guide their children in building relationships among themselves and others. Parents' relationships with others outside their family can impact their children. They have both the right and responsibility to monitor their children's choice of exposure to social media and "games" that shape children's behavioral patterns.

They must raise their children in the context of faith and teach religious values by their credible lifestyle. Their own choices in daily life must reflect their faith and religious values. Children definitely learn from what they feel, see, understand and interact with their parents. Their exercise of Christian faith and charity begins and grows at home. **(9)**

Sylvain-Marie Giraud, in his book, *The Spiritual Exercises of Our Lady of La Salette*, argues that every Christian must strive to ward off sins and their traps in order to reach Christian perfection in charity. This striving requires repentance from sinful ways such as indulging in inordinate and evil desires and redirection of their lives into the righteous ways, namely mortification of inordinate and evil desires and curbing of concupiscence through persistent prayer. These require *purgation* such as naming, taming and changing inordinate desires as well as eliminating sources of temptations.

• *The Purgative Way*, which is doing penance daily by mortifying inordinate and evil desires in communion with Jesus and the Blessed Mother, helps beginners eventually experience lesser effect of the onslaught of sins and temptations. They eventually become ready to engage in...

• *The Illuminative Way*, which is living in the light of Christ that shines forth from the Crucifix worn by the Blessed Mother during her apparition, that helps foster virtues. With the progress in both Purgative and Illuminative Ways, the practitioners are ready to work on their desire for union with God. It means then that they are already imbued with different virtues. The two ways help them achieve and be ready to practice the Unitive Way.

• *The Unitive Way*, which is the way and the goal of Christian life as it is conveyed in the message and ascension of the Blessed Mother during her apparition, requires all of their human faculties to be employed so that God becomes the center of everything. Even their feelings and thoughts are direct-

Our parishioners gather after Mass at new La Salette Parish Chapel in Haiti

ed towards God alone, without missing necessary things in life either through neglect or forgetfulness. **(10)** The Unitive Way helps practitioners to put Heaven into perspective in everything they do.

God initiates and directs every Christian along the path to Christian perfection and the exercise of the ministry of forgiveness and reconciliation. Norman Theroux argues that God showed his initiative for forgiveness and reconciliation at the apparition of the Blessed Mary to La Salette. Having a great concern for his people and interest in their daily affairs, God sent Mary at La Salette.

This event shows that God indeed meets His people where they are. Mary's message conveys God's love for His people. Her message attests to the presence of God in their daily lives offering forgiveness and reconciliation. (11)

According to Theroux, those who exercise these ministries must imitate both Jesus and Mary to bring others to God. They have to initiate relationships with others with welcoming attitudes and meet people where they are to be effective in their ministry. (12) The ministers of forgiveness and reconciliation not only readily welcome people but also unreservedly and unwaveringly accompany them.

Unfortunately, parents, the first teachers of their children, can some-times neglect or forget their great responsibility of being ministers of forgiveness and reconciliation in family relationships. This reality has its origin in the Garden of Eden where the first human parents sev-ered their relationship with God and the rest of creation. Although God's primordial design for human destiny was impeccable happiness with Him for all eternity, sin entered the human heart through the tricks of the serpent. What really happened afterwards?

David E. Rosage states that first humans personally and freely re-belled against God to the extent of losing their authentic freedom in God's love and their privilege to live in Eden. Their assertion of freedom in their own design that is contrary to God's has perpetual effect in the lives of their offspring. Sadly, all human persons still fall prey to this trap of false freedom that always costs them the freedom of being God's children.

The loving and forgiving God, as faithful as He is to His promise of the Savior, sent His Son to restore broken relationships with Him. As He sent prophets to warn the Israelites of their sins and the need for restoration of relationship with Him by avoiding sins, God in the end sent His Son to forgive the sins of His people and reconcile them with Himself. (13)

We can avoid sin with the help of God's grace. J. N. D. Kelly argues that St. Augustine understood sin as loss of freedom that the holy ones enjoy in Heaven. Sharing only the effects of Original Sin, we have the capacity, Augustine construes, not to sin. The "essence" of Original Sin is to participate in the corrupt choice of Adam and to become co-responsible in the act of sin. Sin, for Augustine, concerns freewill. Humans sin because they freely associate with Adam in his ill-will. And every sin is a regeneration of the occasion where Adam sinned. (14)

RÉVÉREND PÈRE S. M. GIRAUD
— MISSIONNAIRE DE LA SALETTE —

LE LIVRE DES

EXERCICES
SPIRITUELS

DE NOTRE-DAME
DE LA SALETTE

1946

Éditions de la Revue des Alpes, Grenoble

Cover of the 1946 version of
"Le Livre des Exercices Spirituels"
by Fr. Giraud

God prepares us for and perpetuates the works of forgiveness and reconciliation. God sent the Blessed Mother at La Salette to warn people of the danger of sin and invited them to return to God who always forgives and reconciles sinners to Himself. How do we cooperate with God and heed Mary's warning in order to prepare ourselves well to experience God's forgiveness and reconciliation with Him?

What is a Proper Disposition through Penance?

Sylvain-Marie Giraud encourages the practitioners of La Salette Spirituality to dispose themselves properly and do it in three degrees in particular.

Prayer – The First Degree of La Salette Spirituality (The Purgative Way)

The *first degree* requires them to have a contrite heart for having committed sins against God. Since any sin against God and others make the Blessed Mother suffer and cry, they must expiate their sins and loathe mortal sins. They have to be in communion with the weeping Mother by sharing her tears. They have to dispose themselves properly, repent of their sins, and "frequent the sacraments, mental prayer, certain penitential and charitable practices."

Mortification of all inordinate desires in order to see the goodness of God in everything is of great necessity. It is the way of sharing the passion of Christ, of regaining the sight of Heaven, and abhorring the menace of Hell. It also means to live in God's grace and maintain friendship with God. **(15)**

Why do we do spiritual exercises? Theroux's argument would provide the importance of spiritual exercises which helps redirect our lives to God. Theroux argues that God sent Mary at La Salette to reclaim sinners because they are His people. God does abhor sins but loves sinners. God, through Mary at La Salette. invites His people to surrender themselves to His will. Their faithfulness to Him will help them avoid everything that contradicts His will. Their fidelity to Him forms their right attitude towards Him, others and themselves. They eventually are able to realign their lives and live a reconciled life as their will conforms to His.

Theroux reflects on the warnings of Mary against people's unfaithfulness to Sunday obligation and disrespect for Jesus. Their negative attitude towards the Church and God in fact ruins their lives as Children of God. Therefore, Mary invited Christians to redirect their lives on the right path as marked out for them by Jesus. They have to "honor" both Jesus and Sunday **(16)**

What happens to those who do spiritual exercises? Rosage argues that we do spiritual exercises not to earn God's favor but to enable ourselves to admit our own sinfulness and ask God to forgive us. In this way, neither God nor ourselves are forced in receiving and giving forgiveness.

It is that we always need God's help to cleanse us of our sins. Letting God's forgiveness penetrate our hearts means letting God work in our lives. This means that we show God our sorrowful heart and promise to do His will. We do God's will just like Jesus always does. God sees and accepts our properly disposed hearts so much so that His forgiving love purifies and heals us of our sins. (17)

Mary asked: "Do you pray well, my children?"

How do we begin our spiritual exercises? At the outset of this chapter on the three pillars of La Salette Spirituality and Giraud's three ways, it is apt to present first the three pillars of La Salette Spirituality as stated in the Constitution, number 6, of the *Rule of Life* of the Missionaries of Our Lady of La Salette. They are "prayer, penance and zeal" that are mentioned in the message of Our Lady of La Salette. These three pillars help the missionaries to prepare themselves to do the ministry of reconciliation as mandated by Mary during her apparition at La Salette. They live out their mission as witnesses to the message of Our Lady of La Salette. (18)

How important is prayer in Christian life? Why and how should every Christian pray?

Giraud reflects on the importance of prayer as emphasized by Mary at La Salette during her conversation with the two children. Prayer is indispensable in Christian life because it is the only way Christians and their God communicate with each other. A Christian lifts his/her soul to God in order to commune with him and asks for whatever is needed in his/her life. A Christian is called to praise and give thanks to God.

A very specific prayer that Mary recommends Christians to pray when they do not have enough time is the Our Father. It is a very simple and doable prayer that Christians can pray regularly and faithfully. God indeed wants Christians to be consistent and incessant in their prayers so that they do not end up communing with someone else other than God their creator and redeemer. Without praying the prayer commanded by God and recommended by Mary, Christians will fall prey to sins and salvation will be out of reach.

Without the help of God through prayer, it is impossible to be saved. Besides, we need God's grace to do everything that concerns our lives. Setting a certain time a day for prayer and praying faithfully at that designated time nourish our souls. When we pray, we imitate Mary who prays unceasingly for us. We pray together with all saints and angels in communion with the whole Church. **(19)**

Whom we pray to and how we pray matter for Christians. Prayer has to be other- oriented. Christian prayer is different from the prayers of the Pharisees. It is directed to God and for the service of others, while those of the Pharisees do otherwise. Jon Sobrino argues that Jesus taught prayer as directed to God so as to correct Pharisaic type of prayer that is egotistic and hedonistic. Jesus instilled in the minds and hearts of people to pray in a "correct" and practical way.

Jesus taught us that prayer has to be married with action because it opens up the entrance to God's presence and paves the way to service of the needy. That's the reason behind the early Christians' avoidance of "spiritual narcissism, hypocrisy, wordiness, and alienating and oppressive misuse of prayer, and sensationalism." **(20)**

The very reason Mary asked Maximin and Melanie if they ever prayed well was that there are many obstacles in prayer life. Proper prayers are necessary for productive works. Praying well is indispensable in making important decisions in life. It is much more important especially in doing the ministry of forgiveness and reconciliation, which are divine attributes. Furthermore, forgiveness and reconciliation can be carried out only with the help of God. They are the works of God who initiates every good thing for right relationship with Him and with everyone. Jesus shows us the example.

Sobrino argues that Jesus' life is imbued with prayer. Jesus began and ended His public ministry with prayers. He had both a personal and communal prayer life because He would often pray in solitude as well as join community prayers in synagogues. Jesus prayed before curing and healing the sick, performing miracles, driving out evil spirits and making life-changing decisions. Whenever He prayed, as opposed to the way Pharisees did, He praised and thanked the Father for everything the Father provides.

Icon of Sts. Cyprian of Carthage and Justina, martyred in 304ad; photo: Biso

Furthermore, He entrusted everything to the will of the Father for He knows it is not about Himself but about the Father and the people he was sent to save. The Father indeed is a relational God with whom Jesus Himself and all of God's children can personally and concretely communicate. (21) As Jesus Himself engaged in both personal and communal prayers, the early Christians also practiced the same forms of prayers as guided and taught by their leaders.

Agnes Cunningham, in her book, *Prayer: Personal and Liturgical*, presents how the early fathers construed and taught prayer. Still rooted in Jewish theology of prayer, prayer for the early Christians is "a peti-tion" (Augustine), conversation with God (John Chrysostom), "a spo-ken reason" (Cassiodorus), and asking for "becoming things of God" (John Damascene). Clement of Rome specifically speaks of prayer as asking for God's forgiveness for our sins. The point of departure or development from Jewish tradition came only with the writing of Tertullian on prayer (*De Oratione*). His writing provides three compo-nents that are basically drawn from those of Christ: "the spirit where-by it can have such power, the word by which it is expressed, and the reason why it produces reconciliation." In the light of the way Jesus prays, Tertullian's teaching on prayer emphasizes how a true spirit of prayer, a true expression and a reason for praying are essential for a prayer to bring about reconciliation. Tertullian believes that Christ brought a new dimension to prayer to the extent that it becomes part and parcel of every Christian's life as the Our Father characterizes it. **(22)**

According to Agnes Cunningham, Tertullian taught that in praying the Our Father "we adore God and affirm our faith." It is also praying for the will of God to be done in us and everyone. Praying this prayer reminds us of the fulness of God's will that enables us to become His children and provides us with everything we need. Furthermore, this prayer calls us to imitate His actions that fulfill the will of the Father. We pray the Our Father that our sins be forgiven and have the grace to avoid sins. **(23)**

Pope Benedict XVI, in his encyclical letter, *Spe Salvi* (*On Christian Hope*), teaches that praying the Our Father and the Hail Mary alone and with the Church purifies and prepares our inner self to be open to God and others. Prayer must be "constantly guided and enlight-ened by the great prayers of the Church and the saints, by liturgical prayer, in which the Lord teaches us again and again how to pray properly. Cardinal Nguyen Van Thuan, in his book of Spiritual Exercises, tells us that during his life there were long periods when he was unable to pray and that he would hold fast to the texts of the Church's prayer: the Our Father, the Hail Mary and the prayers of the liturgy." **(24)**

Jesus taught His disciples how to pray in the following words, which is called the Our Father:

> "Our Father in heaven, hallowed be your name, your kingdom come, your will be done, on earth as in heaven. Give us today our daily bread; and forgive us our debts, as we forgive our debtors; and do not subject us to the final test; but deliver us from the evil one" (Matthew 6:9-13)

The Hail Mary is one of the prayers we will be discussing. The following text is taken from the archives of the United States Conference of Catholic Bishops:

> "Hail Mary, full of grace, the Lord is with you; blessed are you among women, and blessed is the fruit of your womb, Jesus. Holy Mary, Mother of God, pray for us sinners now and at the hour of our death" (CCC 2676-2677).

We shall see how Mary at La Salette insisted on praying well, especially the Our Father and the Hail Mary. The La Salette *Rule of life* states that Mary reminded the children to develop a habit of a personal prayer life as well as to engage in ecclesial prayer life. They have to pray at least twice a day, that is, morning and evening. If they don't have time, they have to pray at least an Our Father and a Hail Mary. She also said that it is necessary to say prayers of intercession on behalf of others:

Our Lady of La Salette asked the children: "*Do you say your prayers well, my children?*" "Hardly ever, Madam," the two shepherds answered candidly. "*Ah, my children, you should say them well, at night and in the morning, even if you say only an Our Father and a Hail Mary when you can't do better. When you can do better, say more.*"

Mary's emphasis on the Our Father echoes instruction given even in the patristic times.

Cunningham argues that it was Origen, a third-century Christian scholar (184-253ad), who developed a more systematic definition of prayer. Origen contends that to pray is to appeal, praise, intercede and give thanks to God. As the early Christian community grew in number, the Our Father became a more intimate and normative prayer Christians prayed addressing God as their Father. They prayed this prayer as Jesus addressed the Father in the most intimate way by calling him, *Abba*. They prayed the Our Father regularly, especially at "morning, noon, evening, and midnight."

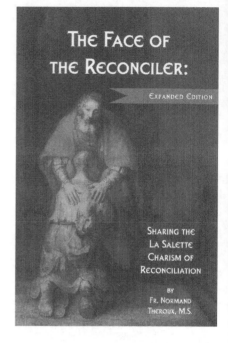

THE FACE OF
THE RECONCILER:

EXPANDED EDITION

SHARING THE
LA SALETTE
CHARISM OF
RECONCILIATION

BY
FR. NORMAND
THEROUX, M.S.

To better understand the importance and power of this prayer, we may read Pope Francis's invitation to all Christians to pray it for the end of the Coronavirus Pandemic – a respiratory illness that was first identified in Wuhan city, Hubei Province, China and reported to the World Health Organization on December 31, 2019. It was declared a global health emergency on December 30, 2019 and a global pandemic on March 11, 2020.

Christopher Wells, in his article, "Pope Francis Announces Extraordinary *Urbi et Orbi* Blessing," said that Pope Francis asked all Christians around the world to pray the Our Father together with him at noontime of March 25, 2020. The pope insisted that God will hear the united prayer of all Christians. Seeking God's help is necessary to bring about protection and healing from the Coronavirus pandemic. **(25)**

After reflecting on the necessity of prayer, Sylvain-Marie Giraud deals with the way Christians should pray. The *first prerequisite* for a good prayer based on what Mary said at La Salette is asking only something that salvation necessitates. Mary's message on how to pray has a definitive tone because she speaks of the indispensable nature of praying well. Any prayer well-prayed shall not be without any answer. She even spoke of how a sincere prayer from the heart would change *"If they are converted, rocks and stones will turn into heaps of wheat, and potatoes will be self-sown in the fields."*

We see how intentionally directing our prayers to God helps us acquire the *second prerequisite* for prayer called "fervor" that is accompanied by "faith, hope and charity." Giraud asserts that faith is needed in praying because nothing that pertains to salvation can be done without it. Hope is also necessary because it assures and convinces us that our prayers shall be answered. All answered prayers bear a fruit called charity. To be charitable means that one is in God's grace. As prayer is needed for us to be in God's grace, we can't pray without the grace of God or sustain faith, hope and charity. **(26)**

The reason why Giraud highlights the role of faith, hope and charity is well explained by the Fathers of the Church in their writings on the meaning of the Our Father. Cunningham explains that Tertullian also focuses on how our belief is expressed in the Father whose will alone is the sole intention of our prayers. We pray well when we do it with love for Him only whom we obey. God wills that all of His children are saved as attested by Abraham, the father of faith.

Origen emphasizes the sense of trust every Christian must have in God the Father as Jesus has. The relationship between God's children and God himself is strengthened and expressed in the Our Father. The eschatological aspect of our relationship with God is made manifest in it, too. Communion with all the saints is proclaimed as well.

The Good Shepherd logo adapted from a Christian tombstone in the Catacombs of Domitilla in Rome.

Cyprian of Carthage (210-258ad) goes even further claiming that when we pray the Our Father, even in private, we do it in communion with the pilgrim Church throughout the world and the triumphant Church in Heaven. **(27)**

This simple prayer unites us with God, saints and angels, and the whole Church. Ralph Martin, in his book, *The Fulfillment of All Desire*, recounts the witness of St. Theresa of Avila to the experience of one of her sisters being in "the highest state of union by reciting the Our Father with attention and openness to the Spirit's presence." In this prayer, we "respond to and nurture" our relationship with God by entering His mind and praying well. **(28)**

Cunningham claims that Gregory of Nyssa tirelessly preached to Christians on praying well so as to recondition themselves and maintain the image of God within. The Our Father taught by Jesus is the model of all prayers in praising God as well as fighting against temptations. This prayer helps us transcend temporal realities and transform our physical body to be in communion with God. It aids us to long for and adhere to unchanging realities that exit because of God's infinitely pure will.

Praying this prayer acknowledges the power of God that brings back into our lives "balance and harmony" that sins have destroyed. Gregory of Nyssa fondly calls Jesus the Divine Physician for He cures the disease of sins in our lives. Jesus delivers us from the evil ones and their web of temptations and sins and gives us this powerful prayer to guard us against temptations. This prayer helps us know whom we pray to, what we pray for and who saves us. **(29)**

Brendan Byrne, in his commentary on the Our Father in the Gospel of Matthew (6:9-15), argues that it begins with lifting up the human spirit from personal cares that weigh a person down to the freedom of the Father in Heaven. Jesus through the prayer forms family spirit by bringing them into the intimate and trusting relationship He has with his Father. Jesus breaks His followers free from the captivity of the evil ones and their kingdom by calling down His Kingdom. Only God's will, not that of the evil one, shall be done so that everything his followers need for their survival and salvation shall be granted to them.

As they journey in this life till they reach the Kingdom of Heaven, they always need to be continually forgiven. God's forgiveness flows to make human forgiveness grow. However, the human dimension can curtail the divine attribute. The believers pray that God may protect them from the onslaught of the evil ones and help them to combat and overcome temptations daily. **(30)**

Cunningham argues that Cyril of Jerusalem explains how good and great God is in the lives of saints and in the whole of His creation. Cyril also commented on the nature of temptations and the power of this prayer against temptations in order that Christians understand and overcome them. Cyril compared Peter who was like a good swimmer and Judas who drowned in the sea of temptations and sins. We ask the Lord through the Our Father to defend us against and deliver us from our perpetual enemy, the devil itself. **(31)**

Giraud reechoes the necessity of prayer as taught by the Fathers of the Church and reminded by Mary at La Salette. Every Christian is responsible to pray daily. We offer everything to the Lord and do every good thing in communion with the whole Church. In that is included prayer. When we pray in the name of the Trinity and invoke the names of the departed holy men and women, we pray with the whole Church.

Fr. Marcel Schlewer, M.S., theologian, author and retreat director

We pray for the Church because we pray for those who do not pray for any reason and for those in the suffering Church. **(32)** Also how often we pray does matter in this busy age of ours. We begin the day rushing, running and sometimes ruining the joy of the day due to many tasks we have to finish up.

Normand Theroux, in his book, The Face of the Reconciler: Sharing the La Salette Charism of Reconciliation, speaks of how Mary reminded us to pray twice a day so that everything that occurs throughout the day shall be entrusted to the Lord's guidance and protection. Since forgiveness and reconciliation are the work of God, the ministers of reconciliation have to be in constant communication with the Lord. Prayer keeps ministers of reconciliation in God's grace-filled moment and "environment."

Mary at La Salette emphasizes the indispensability of prayer because it maintains our presence and even those of people who don't or cannot pray in God's "presence." Everything of the day has to be imbued with God's grace to the extent that the evil one has no space in it. A regular, consistent, and perseverant prayer has to be made into a "habit" so that a lifetime character shall be formed. This long and lasting way of life shall be the most impactful witness to the message of Mary. (33) Although we know it is part and parcel of Christian life to pray, what prayers we say also matter!

Giraud believes that Mary wants to make our prayers as practical and "perfect as possible." She teaches us to begin our prayer life with something simple and doable. This simple prayer can be found in the common and universal prayers of the Church such as the Our Father and the Hail Mary. She wants us to pray these prayers regularly and meditatively as part of our daily life. She always speaks of her Son Jesus and his Church so that we pray with a good intention and attitude. We are responsible to return to God together with all our brothers and sisters. That's the essence of her apparition at La Salette. (34) Prayer helps us see the light in Christ. This light shining from Christ on the Cross shows us the way. It illuminates the path that leads to forgiveness and reconciliation. This light that helps God's children return to him will be explained more in the Illuminative Way.

Robert Spitzer, in his book, Five Pillars of the Spiritual Life: A Practi-

cal Guide to Prayer for Active People, recommends that we pray simple prayers. One simple, fundamental prayer is the Hail Mary that asks the Blessed Mother to console, understand and accompany us in our daily life both in good and bad times. Simple and spontaneous prayers help us entrust to God everything, while we do our best. This evokes God's guidance that transforms us to let God take care of our lives.

With God in control, we are able to forgive ourselves and others, while we forgo whatever doesn't conform to our identity as God's children. The grace of forgiveness is granted to us so that we are free to forgive ourselves and others. This gift of forgiveness readies us to accept God's gift of reconciliation in the Holy Spirit who is our primordial aid in prayers. **(35)** These two prayers – the Our Father and the Hail Mary – sustain us in God's reconciling love and help us avoid sins as well as attain God's forgiveness.

The Purgative Way

Christians are called to imitate Jesus in undergoing life's sufferings. Mary at La Salette wept and invited God's children to return to God by praying, doing penance and having zeal for God daily. Penance, which is one of the pillars of La Salette spirituality, can help us better understood Giraud's purgative way.

Penance, a Pillar of La Salette Spirituality

Before we go to this particular pillar of La Salette spirituality, it is helpful to have a better understanding of what penance means in Christian spirituality. James Dallen states that St. Augustine, one of the Church Fathers, taught everyday penance. According to Augustine, all Christians by virtue of baptism should do penance on a daily basis for the rest of their lives. Praying the Our Father is fundamental in doing penance. Aside from praying this particular prayer, they can also fast, or give alms as a sign of penance for the forgiveness of sins. **(36)**

J. N. D. Kelly, in his book, *Early Christian Doctrines*, argues that St. Augustine taught early Christians to pray, fast and give alms as their daily penances. Doing these acts of penance would gain them the forgiveness of their sins and reconciliation with God. St. Augustine taught penance as part of every Christian's daily spiritual life so that they would be worthy to receive God's forgiveness and reconciliation and those of the believing community. Penance requires a person's whole being, all human faculties, to be active as much as possible. **(37)**

The Catechism of the Catholic Church teaches that "penance requires ... the sinner to endure all things willingly, be contrite of heart, confess with the lips, and practice complete humility and fruitful satisfaction" (CCC, 1450). It "consists of prayer, an offering, works

La Salette Weeping Mother, the first of three phases of the Apparition

of mercy, service of neighbor, voluntary self-denial, sacrifices, and above all the patient acceptance of the cross we must bear" (CCC, 1460). Understanding penance in the context of Christian spirituality, we shall now see it through the lenses of Giraud's purgative way.

Giraud argues that the purgative way corresponds to the first degree of spiritual life for it deals with sin and its malice. To sin means to refuse to submit to the will of God. It is a rebellion against God, and living a life against His will disrupts order in life. Mary reminds us in her message that people's continuous refusal of God's invitation for right relationship with Him makes the burden she carries heavier day after day.

Turning away from God and His ways means living our lives in our own ways, even to the point of openly doing things that are contrary to the Church's teachings on fasting and abstinence. For this very reason, Mary at La Salette reprimands those who prefer "butcher shops" to churches. She said: "*In Lent they go to the butcher shops like dogs.*" Mary used stern words to warn God's people against dangers that sins bring into their lives, particularly the loss of God's grace. The absence of grace disables one to be good and to do good. The worst thing is that sins debase and enslave them. **(38)**

Turning away from God means turning away from our true selves, too. We prefer our own will to the will of God. It is worse to do the will of fallen angels. But, how can one become aware of the evil one's traps and avoid them? As everything has an origin and history of development, so does every sin. Giraud argues that sinners' willful and voluntary refusal to do God's will can be compared to the willful rebellion of the fallen angels. Every sin one commits is in fact following the order of the evil one that always contradicts God and all of His good will for us. **(39)** Giraud, 66)

Mary during her apparition spoke of people's refusal to submit their lives to God. We submit our lives either to temptations of the self, the world and the evil one or to the truths of our faith and the love of God. Our use of our God-given freedom can either endanger our dignity as God's image and identity as followers of Christ or engender our growth in faith and love of God. But, how do people refuse God's will or disobey him anyway?

Marcel Schlewer, M.S., in his book, *All My People: Why She Spoke-Why*

She Wept at La Salette, argues that people's misuse of freedom costs them their obedience to God's will. The assertion of freedom in their own design – that is, doing whatever they want, especially in the practice of religion – has its origin even in the Garden of Eden where our first human parents committed the first sin. They failed to see how their refusal to submit themselves to God causes disharmony in their lives.

> Mary said: "*If my people refuse to submit, I will be forced to let go the arm of my Son. It is so strong and so heavy, I can no longer hold it back.*"

Mary's invitation to submission to God is to reconcile with God in order to restore harmony in their lives. Mary pointed out how human disobedience even affects other parts of God's creation. Although entrusted to human care, the whole of creation is subject to their use, misuse, abuse. Mary came to warn us against the misuse and abuse of our freedom and resources. Mary came to warn us against God's judgement. Mary came to remind us that the Father entrusted everything to the Son so that everything will return to him through Christ. We all are included in the divine plan of returning to God. (40) Mary's apparition tells us that God never gives up on sinners.

Norman Theroux explains that God loves sinners although He abhors sins. For this reason, Mary appeared at La Salette to remind us of the need to submit ourselves to God's will. His will is that we do every-thing that builds and sustains our relationship with Him. God wills to reconcile with us even if our sins break our relationship with Him. In the process of reconciliation, God helps us realign our lives back on the right track to give us the fullness of life in Him. Mary came to bring us into the awareness of conforming to God's will in our daily life so that we will have the fullness of life. (41) How do people faith-fully submit to God's will?

Schlewer contends that submission to Christ is the only way to find meaning in life. We have to submit ourselves to Christ who is at work in all of us through the power of the Holy Spirit. Mary at La Salette mentioned the necessity of our submission to Christ who submitted Himself to the Father and regained everything for us. Mary reminds us that our submission to Christ has an effect both on our lives and the whole of creation, just as sins affect us all and everything in life. We must avoid sins that distance us from God and make us lose our way to Him. Christians have the responsibility to renew all things in Christ and help others return to God. **(42)**

Peter Fink, in his article, "Investigating the Sacrament of Penance: An Experiment in Sacramental Theology," argues that God initiates through Jesus Christ a turn to humans who in turn approach God through the same Jesus. Only when they are united with Jesus can they admit their sins and be forgiven. The reason is that God, out of His love, forgives sins that affect one's faith life and relationships. Sinners strongly resist the human "ability to say yes" to their own lives and fail to "make God's yes" work in their lives. **(43)**

Giraud contends that one's refusal to submit oneself to the loving God allows oneself to participate in the "revolt against God." This revolt against God has its origin in the evil one who revolted against God (Jeremiah 2:20 and 2 Peter 2:4). It seeks its followers by tempting them to believe solely in their own abilities and disregard God's help. It recruits new members in many different ways to assault God's children and God Himself. Awareness and avoidance of its tricks and traps enable God's children to avoid sins and overcome its snares. This sin against God in fact springs from people's contemptuous attitude towards God's infinite and forgiving love, too.

The "contempt for God" forces God's love out of their lives. This leads them into sins that alienate them from God and one another. Sin such as contempt for God worsens broken relationships and widens the gap between God and them and among themselves.

The sin that injures God the most, Giraud argues, is a mortal sin because it outrightly rebels against God. This sin in effect rejects His love that alone gives and sustains our life in Him. This is the reason why Mary wept at La Salette. She wept for the sins of people that offend God. Her apparition calls every sinner to ask for God's forgiveness and reconcile with Him and others. **(44)**

There are reasons, Giraud contends, why people reject God and falter in their faith life. First, people are tepid because despite all the warnings from God through the course of nature, most of them do not care. Insensitivity to God's presence in simple matters harden their hearts even to the point of disregarding simple things and neglecting God's abundant grace. The end result of these is building up habits that contradict God's will.

Eventually, pride which is the root cause of every sin, thrives in the hearts of many. Pride forces people not only to refuse to see God and remain in his love but also take for granted the importance of temperance and purity of heart. This is why Mary said that people indulge in eating meat even in Lent, let alone fail to do regular abstinence in daily life. **(45) Giraud**, 73-75)

Mary's warning against the impending danger due to sins are as strong or almost as strong as those of the prophets Amos and John the Baptist. Marcel Schlewer argues that Mary made very strong remarks on the attitude of the people towards abstinence. Mary compared those who didn't abstain from meat in Lent with dogs. Mary used these words to allude to pagan practices. Lent indeed challenges Christians to be more careful with the way they live their Christian lives. The attitude and actions that lead to sins have to be shunned in order to live their lives in Christ. Mary reminds us that Christ calls all sinners to repentance, forgiveness and reconciliation that culminate in Sundays and the Easter celebration. **(46) Schlewer**, 113-115)

God always takes the initiative to restore His children's love for Him and help fulfill their responsibilities as God's children. Despite many a substitute for Him and His will that comes into the lives of His children, God offers ways and means to draw them back to Himself. In order to bring His people back to Himself, God sent Mary at La Salette. She came to warn them against the danger of breaking holy days of obligation, especially Sundays.

Mary, speaking as a prophet, says: "*I gave you six days to work; I kept the seventh for myself, and no one will give it to me. This is what makes the arm of my Son so heavy.*"

"... I have given you Six days to work ..."

Mary said: "I gave you six days...",
window from Mary Keane Chapel, Enfield, New Hampshire

The *La Salette Rule of Life* reechoes what Mary said at La Salette regarding holy days of obligation, especially Sundays. During her apparition at La Salette, Mary on behalf of Jesus, like the prophets of old did, said that God gives us weekdays to work and to reserve weekends for him. **(47)** People's refusal to have time for God is also their refusal to receive God's offer of his forgiveness and reconciliation.

Giraud argues that such a refusal is tantamount to offending God. We have to be thankful to Him for His wondrous deeds through our observance of holy days of obligation that help us receive the gifts of forgiveness and reconciliation. Furthermore, the Holy Sacrifice of the Mass is the ultimate expression of God's love. The Mass celebrates His Son's suffering, death and resurrection. The Mass also celebrates the victory over sin and death. It is there we share everything of Jesus' life, death and resurrection.

We have gratitude for the three persons of the Trinity. The Holy Spirit teaches us to love God and others above other things. The Holy Spirit also empowers us to resist the enticement of evil spirits, particularly swearing. Mary at La Salette also warned against the danger of swearing, especially by using the name of Jesus. **(48)**

> Mary said: "*And those who drive the carts cannot swear without throwing in my Son's name. These are the two things that make the arm of my Son so heavy.*"

"Those who drive the carts cannot swear wiithout bringing in my Son's name.."

Mary said: "Those who drive the carts cannot swear..."

The *La Salette Rule of Life* states that evil and human spirits teach us everything that contradicts God and His ways. Every sin and swearing done by God's children, make Mary suffer. For this reason, she specifically said that "*those who drive the carts cannot swear without throwing in her Son's name.*" Giraud construes that Mary appeared at La Salette to bring people back to God by reminding them of God's grace of forgiveness and reconciliation.

Mary, as every mother would do for her children, and Jesus who wept for Lazarus, wept for the fate of God's people. Mary teaches us to weep over our sins and those of others so that we may be spared from the judgement of God. The image Mary used to connote the punishment God might bring upon all sinners was *"the arm of her Son."* This biblical image alludes to those used in the Book of Wisdom (11:21; 16:15-16) and the Gospel of Luke (1:51). **(49)** Mary warned us to avoid sins and swearing to be able to avail ourselves of God's forgiveness and reconciliation.

> Mary said: *"If the harvest is ruined, it is only on account of yourselves. I warned you last year with the potatoes. You paid no heed."*

Mary also warned people of signs that point to sins. Sins affect God's creation first as a sign of warning for people so that they may ask for God's forgiveness and reconciliation and change their way of life. Giraud highlights that sinners bring judgement upon themselves. Their sins force God out of their life. Sins cost them the grace of God without which nothing good can happen to them. Because of sins, every bad thing accelerates, to fall upon them. Losing God because of sins means losing the very source of everything humans need in life. Giraud reiterates how Mary spoke of God's way of chastising sinners through "the loss of crops, death and famine." **(50)**

Giraud argues that God uses his creation to remind us of the menace of sins. His creation protests against human infidelity to God. It also decries human activities and lifestyles that waste God's grace and resources for their own insatiable selfish human desires. God's creation also suffers because of the sins of humans, while God's Son suffers with the sinners for the remission of their sins. God does everything in order to bring us back to Himself after we accept His forgiveness and reconciliation. God gives us in many ways temporal punishments in order to save us from the snares of the devil and eternal punishment. **(51)**

Next, Giraud presents the three things that lead everyone to sin. *First,* it is "the desire of the flesh." It causes sickness of any kind physically, psychologically and spiritually if it is not tamed and properly used. *Second* is "the desire of the eyes" which makes us crave for things inordinately. And the worst comes when we covet the things of others. *Third* is "the pride of life" that asks for unnecessary achievements and ambitions. It pushes us to fulfil them even at the expense of the rights of others and limited resources.

Mary said: "*If I want my Son not to abandon you, I am obliged to plead with him constantly.*"

Lamentation **by Pietro Lorenzetti, (1280-1348), Assisi Basilica**

In order to be saved, Giraud argues, we have to die to all things that don't conform to the will and teachings of Jesus. As we share His suffering and death by virtue of our baptism, we have to pattern our lives to His in order to become victorious with Him over sins and death. Mary at La Salette said that she intercedes for us all the time so that Jesus will not abandon us. **(52)**

Jesus suffered and died for us all. In his sufferings and death, Jesus did the most exemplary penance of all. Mary also did penance by pleading to her Son and weeping for all sinners. Emma Anderson argues that Mary at La Salette invites Christians to learn to suffer for others as a sign of reparation for others' sins. As she suffered for sinners by pleading with her Son, she invites every Christian to return to God by redirecting their lives to him through forgiveness and reconciliation. Our interior or spiritual suffering is essential in imitating Mary and Jesus. **(53)**

Despite God's warnings through Mary, Giraud argues, many are still spiritually blind. This heedlessness pushes God out of their lives until they drift further away from God. God's people have their own wrong doings that discard the grace of God. In spite of God's persistence to reconcile with them, they resist God's offer of reconciliation. Their resistance to God's initiative for reconciliation rejects God's everlasting reward. This rejection makes the heart of every sinner hardened. A hardened heart gets worse eventually as it refuses to accept and live in God's grace. The end result is that evil takes root, while the good takes flight. **(54)**

Giraud and the La Salette Crucifix

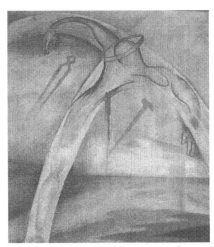

Stylized La Salette crucifix by Argentinian, Fr. Alfredo Velarde, M.S.

Giraud contends that La Salette spirituality emphasizes penance which the Purgative Way elaborates. Mary at La Salette wore the Crucifix upon which was hung the suffering Jesus. The very words of Mary, her tears and the crucifix she wore show how excessive the pain sins cause Jesus. Mary's tears at La Salette vividly expressed the pain of Jesus' sufferings on the road to Calvary and his hanging on the cross until His last breath.

The torment inflicted with tortures upon Jesus by His executioners and the passive response of the onlookers are unbearable even by imagination. Nevertheless, Jesus endured His sufferings and pains for the sake of sinners out of His greatest love for us. Mary's apparition and her message let us know that Jesus' love for us is the only reason he suffered and died. Jesus wants us not to experience the pain of ridicule, humiliation, abandonment, and condemnation both here and hereafter.

It is God's love that makes Jesus freely and lovingly accept everything he suffered so that we in turn may undergo pains and sufferings in life, with joy and freedom for our own sake and those of others. We should weep because of our struggles to avoid sins and overcome temptations rather than let God and Mary weep for our sins again. **(55)**

The Purgative Way, Giraud construes, helps us to look at what sins can do to us, others, creation, and God. It aids us to examine our conscience in a more strict and thorough way so that we may be ready to ask for forgiveness from and reconcile with God. We cannot run and turn away from sins unless we know the disgust and dreadfulness they bring into our lives and those around us.

But Mary in her apparition reminds us that we are never alone because both Jesus and she journey with us. They try to free us from the snares of the evil one and its enslavement. Her message enlightens us to see the dark side of sins and the bright side of grace. She invites us to reconcile with God by returning to Him and turning away from sins. She also asks us to persevere in God's grace so that God's glory may increase in our lives and our salvation will be achieved in the end. To be in God's grace means to have God in our lives. Mary makes this happen since she shares the ministry of reconciliation.

She indeed is the reconciler, second only to Jesus her Son. St. Bernard and St. Germanus of Constantinople attest to it. Mary intercedes for us to be forgiven by and reconciled with God because she has the power against the devil and its domain. Needless to say, then, that she has the power to direct us to her Son Jesus. She does these things through her incessant prayers for sinners. **(56)**

Forsaking our own will as a preparation to acknowledge our sins and accept God's will requires lots of penance in relation to the first degree where contrition is necessary. Giraud explains what has to be done for proper disposition in the second degree.

Penance –The Second Degree of La Salette Spirituality (The Illuminative Way)

The *second degree* entails our doing of penance which requires us to spurn our sins of the past and shun them "in the future."

The most important thing is to undergo pains, trials and temptations to fulfill the desire of God for us. This degree helps us remit our debt to God's goodness and atone for our sins. As Jesus' passion was offered for the sins, and redemption of the world, the unending passion of everyone is for the sins and reconciliation of others with God. This degree resonates with the passion of Mary on Calvary and La Salette. (57)

> Our Lady of La Salette said: "*How long a time I have suffered for you! If I want my Son not to abandon you, I am obliged to plead with him constantly. And as for you, you pay no heed!* "

Church of the Holy Sepulcher in Old Jerusalem where the visitor can touch the place where Jesus died; photo: adriatikus

We do penance not only for ourselves but also for others who do not or cannot do it for themselves. Therefore, the La Salette *Rule of Life* recounts the reason Mary told Maximin and Melanie that she has suffered long enough for the salvation of all, although no one really heeds it. Mary continues to insist that all of us do penance for the remission of sins and reconciliation of sinners with God even if or when people do not like or cannot do anything. Our daily chores such as cleaning our own rooms, throwing the trash away properly, taking care of the sick and the elderly can become our penances for others and for the love of God.

Normand Theroux, M.S., also contends that ministers of reconciliation have to live a life of penance. They have to imitate Mary who implored God's forgiveness for the sins of Christians even to the point of shedding tears at La Salette. Mary even used strong words to point out the seriousness of sins people have been committing. Sins like eating meat in Lent and mockery of religion make Mary suffer for sinners.

Mary at La Salette brought up the indispensability of penance in daily life. She encourages Christians to do penance with joy for it is part and parcel of an authentic Christian living. Christians have to do penance both for themselves and others as the need arises. Doing penance for others signifies our love for them in and among whom Christ is present. **(58)**

Giraud contends that there are two types of penance - passive and active. The passive one, he construes, is done out of one's own choice because here one freely accepts the vicissitudes of life with patience and joy for the salvation of others. A person who does this kind of penance realizes that what she/he suffers is nothing compared to God's justice and punishment. God's anger can have more devasting impact than the pain of one's penance for one's own sins and those of others. The active penance is solely determined by one's will to initiate it. It obliges practitioners' faithfulness and honesty to fast and abstain as the Church teaches. It requires voluntary action to mortify one's desires to be able to master them gradually. To deny oneself is the key to the faithfulness and completion of "active penance." **(59)** Self-denial indeed is very challenging because it requires all human faculties to cooperate with one another.

Zeal –The Third Degree of La Salette Spirituality (The Unitive Way)

Giraud proposes a *third degree* that helps practitioners make proper disposition for "reparation." "Immolation is the major means of reparation. Oblation naturally precedes immolation." In this degree, we reflect Jesus' life and sacrifice as the ultimate recompense for our sins. Practitioners must be humble and able to surrender themselves to Jesus and his Mother and share their passion. In that way, they immolate whatever is yet to be completed in the passion of Christ. They undergo trials and temptations unceasingly and joyfully. Giraud construes that Mary as the Mother of Jesus shares the sufferings of her son. Any kind of recompense practitioners do is sharing the sacrifice and suffering of Jesus and Mary as well as Jesus' victory over sin and death. (60) Share the passion of Jesus and Mary so as to share their glory.

Jean Jaouen, M.S., explains how deep the pain is that Mary must endure for sinners. He argues that every sacrifice we make and suffering we undergo for the sake of Christ and others is not without any merit. We definitely participate in the mission of Christ by sharing his passion and that of Mary even though we can never fully make restitution for all sufferings and pains Jesus and Mary have endured. He contends that this is the very reason Mary at La Salette said that no one will ever recompense the pains she has endured as she pleads with Jesus for the forgiveness of sins. (61) Every parent must be ready to share the pains of Jesus in the exercise of their ministry of forgiveness and reconciliation.

Face of the bronze statues on the Holy Mountain, showing Mary's constant and heartfelt tears at La Salette

Emma Anderson, in her article, "Changing Devotional Paradigms and their Impact upon Nineteenth-Century Marian Apparitions: The Case of La Salette," explains how God and the Blessed Mother suffer with their children. Biblical and historical events attest to God's suffering with His children. Historical events are evident in the whole of Europe, more specifically after the apparition of the Blessed Mother at La Salette on September 19, 1846. Her message at La Salette shows that every suffering their children undergo is linked to those of God and the Blessed Mother. Human suffering if linked to Jesus' sufferings can repair relationships between God and His people as well as the relationships among His people themselves. Sufferings help actualize the redemption wrought by Jesus Christ. **(62)**

God as the initiator of forgiveness and reconciliation through Mary at La Salette invites ministers of forgiveness and reconciliation to undergo pain and suffering in the footsteps of Jesus Christ. The sufferings of the Son of God for the sake of others is the bulwark of an indubitable fact that is necessary for the ministry of forgiveness and reconciliation. Giraud's approach to La Salette spiritual practices explains why we undergo suffering and how well we can do it faithfully.

Prayer, penance and the Purgative Way prepare us to contemplate Jesus who illumines our lives. The crucifix the Blessed Mother wore at her apparition attests to the fact that Jesus illumines our lives. Mary Fabyan Windeatt, in her book, *The Children of La Salette*, describes what Mary looked like and what she wore so as to impress upon the two children the significance of her apparition. One of the things that caught the attention of the children was "an eight-inch crucifix, with a hammer on one crossbar and pincers on the other" around the neck of Mary. **(63)**

Schlewer reflects on the fullness of redemption which the cross of Christ brought about. The cross bears signs of Jesus' suffering and death. The sufferings and pains Jesus endured are part of discipleship as St. Paul and many martyrs in every generation have witnessed. Mary invites whoever looks at the La Salette cross to stand with those who suffer in every age. The cross was the brightest thing she was wearing. The cross caught the attention of the children.

The cross also reminds us of the most obvious signs of our times – sufferings from hunger, violence and diseases. It teaches us to see life's vicissitudes in the light of the Resurrected Christ. The resplendent light coming from the cross illumines and emboldens everyone to dare to follow the way of the cross until they reach the day of resurrection. **(64)**

Giraud describes the significance of the cross that was connected to a chain around Mary's neck. On the cross was the image of the body of Christ with a hammer at the left and pincers at the right. This whole image of the cross signifies the suffering and "crucified Christ" who came to save all. **(65)**

Giraud continues to explain that Mary wore the cross upon which her Son hung to tell us that he is "the center at which all things converge and from which all things radiate." The whole of salvation history is all about her Son because it speaks of God's preparing humans for salvation wrought by his Son from the fall to the Incarnation, the Resurrection and the Ascension. Everything salvific the Church has done, is doing and will still do springs from and is geared towards her Son in the unity of the Father and the Holy Spirit. The suffering, death and resurrection of Jesus Christ illumine God's everlasting love for all His people.

Mary wearing the shining crucifix came to remind us of the importance of having Jesus at the center of our lives. Mary who knows her Son perfectly challenges us to acknowledge Jesus as everything. Mary loves her gentle, forgiving and loving Son beyond our imagination. She invites us to love her Son the way she does. Her holiness is as great as her love for Jesus. Her love for Jesus is the reflection of His love for her. **(66)**

The La Salette *Rule of Life* mandates every professed member to have Jesus Christ as the only source and center of their lives. By virtue of profession of three evangelical counsels, members of the community are required to heed the warnings of Mary and follow Jesus who is the center of their lives. Having Christ at the center of their lives definitely helps them live their lives to the fullest (*The Rule of Life*, 7). This is not any human invention but the invitation of Mary at La Salette. We see how every La Salette missionary embraces this *rule of life* as humanly as possible. But what does it really mean to have Jesus at the center of our lives?

Normand Theroux, in his book, *Our La Salette Mission: To Reconcile Her People* with Her Son, focuses on the message of Mary who invites us to have Jesus at the center of our lives. We prioritize Jesus as Mary does, as attested to by her message at La Salette. Jesus becomes the center of our lives as we remain faithful to God through our daily personal prayers and weekly communal prayers.

The former prayer means praying an Our Father and a Hail Mary if we have no sufficient time. The latter means observance of the Sabbath by attending Mass. We show our special love for Jesus and everything He teaches by praying these prayers. We must never forget that Mary sees us the way Jesus does and loves us in the same measure Jesus does. **(67)**

Giraud contends that Mary wearing the crucifix upon which her Son was crucified showed her love for us at La Salette. She invites everyone to never lose Jesus in their lives by turning away from God or turning down every one of his invitations to forgiveness and reconciliation. Christians have to develop a loving attitude towards Jesus so that they may learn to "gaze upon" the image of Jesus Crucified.

The loving gaze of God and our response to it mold us to have love for God and others. Our love for the image of the Crucified Christ on the Cross is made manifest in a concrete and visible manner in

Madonna of Humility
by Fra Angelico (1395-1455).

wearing a crucifix. Therefore, those who love and embrace the Illuminative Way wear a La Salette cross as a precious jewel. **(68)**

What happens to us when we are illuminated by the light of Christ is witnessed by the honest words of Mary at La Salette. Capitular Norm No. 39 states that every minister of forgiveness and reconciliation has to comprehend and imbibe in their lives that sins alienate us from God. They are responsible to eradicate with God's help sins that cause alienation. Ministers of forgiveness and reconciliation avoid sins to reinstate a sense of faith in God in those who have lost faith. Likewise, they help restore the original human dignity that is lost due to sins. They help rediscover and reaffirm the creaturehood of every person so much so that everyone is able to foster humility and grow in it. **(69)**

What is Humility in La Salette Spirituality?

Giraud contends that "the authentic sign of humility is an inner and supernatural leaning which inclines us to withdraw from the sight of others and live a life hidden in God." Or as St. Paul says: "For you have died, and your life is hidden with Christ in God" (Colossian 3:3).

Mary taught us what humility really means for she spoke with all humility, like prophets do, the truth about people's sinful conditions using stern words to warn God's people of the impeding danger sins bring about. Mary came to the level of God's people. She wore simple clothing, as Jesus' clothes in the manger, to symbolize humility against a dominant hedonistic culture.

Mary's humble, simple and modest speech and dress bespeak Christian duty to care for the outcasts of the society. She chose poor and unschooled children as well as a silent and solitude place to bring the message of forgiveness and reconciliation. Therefore, we are invited to remain humble and open in order to receive God's forgiveness and reconciliation. **(70)** Giraud, 145-151)

> Mary said: "*In the winter, when they don't know what to do, they go to Mass just to make fun of religion.*"

Our humility, simplicity and openness to God's forgiving and reconciling love is totally linked to tangible realities of our faith. Giraud here speaks of Mary's rebuke of those who disrespect God and the Eucharist by mocking at religious activities. People mocked at religion when they had nothing to do or can't do anything in times of inclement weather, like winter.

Mary insisted that people have to reform their lives and attitude towards God and religious duties in order to receive God's forgiveness and reconciliation. Heeding the warning of Mary and reparation of their lives will enable them to receive forgiveness and reconciliation and participate in these twin spiritual attributes. These works Christ has done on Calvary are what we were reminded of by Mary at La Salette. (71) The Illuminative Way helps us to see both sinful and holy realities.

Norman Theroux asserts that people's mockery of religion is the problem of every age, due to too much emphasis on the fact that God is a forgiving God. Even priests find it hard to deliver the message of hard truth. They tend to be more and more lenient and easy-going. On the contrary, Mary's message is centered on the Paschal Mystery of Jesus that brought about forgiveness and reconciliation.

The Illuminative Way necessitates minsters of forgiveness and reconciliation to present the whole truth about the reconciling works of God in Jesus life and ministry and to embody the whole work of Christ that brings about forgiveness and reconciliation. Prayer, especially communal prayer in the Eucharist, is central to the life of the whole Church and therefore, to every minister. (72)

The encounter with God in prayer and the Eucharist purifies us to live a worthy life in Christ. Giraud explains that the purity faithful followers of Jesus and practitioners of La Salette spirituality need is vividly manifested by the apparition itself. The surroundings, the visionaries, Mary and her message signify purity.

Everything that is associated with the apparition also revealed the impurity the world has. We see that only children who were not tainted by impurities of the world could encounter Mary, who is sinless and pure. They would even say that she is a very beautiful woman. Maximin later in his life would say the reason he didn't marry was that he could find no woman whose beauty is closest to the quintessential beauty of the Lady who appeared at La Salette.

To both acquire and remain in purity requires purgation even in this earthly life, as we have seen in the Purgative Stage. The children couldn't touch her but their desire to remain with her lasted for the rest of their lives. They wanted to be united with her at the outset of the apparition. **(73)**

Ministers of forgiveness and reconciliation have the duty and responsibility to help restore the original image of every child of God and the world they live in. Then, the question we have to ask must be, "What should we do to respond to Mary's invitation for all to return to God?" Simply put, sharing the gift of forgiveness and reconciliation is the noblest thing to do.

Jean Jaouen, in his book, *A Grace Called La Salette: A Story for the World*, contends that we all must journey together with our brothers and sisters on our pilgrimage. Our witness to God's invitation and co-journeying with others is so crucial because our experience of God's forgiveness and reconciliation has to be shared with others. What we lack in the areas of exercise of forgiveness and reconciliation shall be reinforced by those who have different charisms.

Fr. Jean Jaouen, M.S. (1898-1975), noted author, theologian and historian

For the benefit and growth of the Church, every Christian is a messenger of God's forgiveness and reconciliation as Maximin and Melanie were. God expressed His will through Mary to forgive and reconcile with every sinner. He requires us to renew our hearts and change our lifestyles as Maximin and Melanie did after their encounter with Mary at La Salette. Maximin and Melanie became more prayerful and faithful spreaders of the message of forgiveness and reconciliation after their encounter with Mary. We are duty-bound to share this same message with others. **(74)** This leads us to the Unitive

Way.

The Unitive Way

Imitation of Christ and Mary in doing the ministry of forgiveness
and reconciliation is of the utmost importance. Only with Christ and
Mary can one be a zealous minister as such. In order to understand
Giraud's claim that the Unitive Way is the foundation of the zeal of
every minister of forgiveness and reconciliation, we must see connec-
tion to the third pillar of La Salette spirituality.

Zeal, a Pillar of La Salette Spirituality

The third pillar of La Salette spirituality is apostolic zeal. It calls for
unwavering and faithful commitment and dedication to the ministry
of forgiveness and reconciliation. Donald Paradis, M.S., in his book,
The Missionaries of La Salette: From France to America, notes that the
canonical approval of the Congregation of the Missionaries of Our
Lady of La Salette depended solely on the three pillars of La Salette
spirituality – prayer, penance and zeal. These pillars are distinct
missionary characteristics that enflesh Mary's message of forgiveness
and reconciliation. The three pillars help us to continue to spread the
message of La Salette throughout its history adapting to the ever-
changing landscape of the current times. **(75)**

The need for every minister's simplicity of life, Emma Anderson
argues, in the ministry of forgiveness and reconciliation is well
addressed by the Blessed Mother with her words, gestures and the
visionaries she chose. The message begged a change in the lives of
Christians, especially the leaders of the Church of the time in France.
The simple and the humble are chosen to zealously spread the message of God's forgiveness and reconciliation. Those who embrace the
ministry God entrusts to them have to change their lifestyles into
that of Mary and of Christ so as to become credible ministers of forgiveness and reconciliation. **(76)**

A life of simplicity is essential to remain faithful to the message of

La Salette. St. John Paul II in his address to the Missionaries of Our Lady of La Salette on their 29th General Chapter in 2000 reminded them of their charism, spirituality and mission. The missionaries and their collaborators must continuously be aware that they participate in the mission of reconciliation in communion with the Church. They are instrumental in helping the Church guide her children in accepting God's forgiveness and become witnesses throughout the world (John Paul II, 1). The missionaries themselves are to be guided first before they offer their guidance to others.

Pope St. John Paul II met with the members of the La Salette 2000 General Chapter in Rome

The La Salette *Rule of Life* states:

4) Moved by the Holy Spirit who prompted the Son of God to experience our human condition and die on the cross in order to reconcile the world to his Father we resolve, in the light of the Apparition of Our Lady of La Salette, to be devoted servants of Christ and of the Church for the fulfillment of the mystery of reconciliation.

5) Faithful to our origins we profess a deep love for Mary, Mother of Christ and of the Church. In our apostolate we follow the example of the handmaid of the Lord who was made reconciler particularly at the foot of the cross.

7) Christ is the rule of our life. **(77)**

The La Salette *Rule of Life* guides the Missionaries of Our Lady of La Salette to live their lives after the example of Mary who witnessed

God's forgiveness and reconciliation at the foot of the cross of her Son Jesus on Calvary. Mary at La Salette brought to our attention the centrality of Christ in our lives. She spoke of her Son's will for us to return to God and reconcile with Him.

She reminds us that Jesus' suffering, death and resurrection are the foundation and proof of God's forgiveness and reconciliation. His life and ministry are the source and resource for the missions of the La Salette missionaries. Giraud took Mary's apparition and her emphasis on the role of Christ to create the exercises.

Giraud argues that once we are freed from sin through prayer and purgation and illuminated by the Savior's reconciling love, we are totally forgiven and fully reconciled with ourselves, others and God. The Unitive Way is a fruit of the prayer, penance and illumination. The Unitive Way gives us a glimpse of Heaven on earth and makes us desire more of Heaven. Such a Heavenly reality was already witnessed by the two children at La Salette.

This is also why Jaouen contends that during her apparition, Mary's voice was like "music" that soothed the hearts of the frightened children. The light shone so bright that no shadow ever appeared around her and the children. Mary's voice and the light were glimpses of Heaven. With her loving gaze, Mary "lowered her eyes and leaned slightly towards them" to give the message of forgiveness and reconciliation. She entrusted the message to the children. **(78)**

To understand and live the message of forgiveness and reconciliation, Giraud provides the third way – the Unitive Way or "the way to Heaven." The Unitive Way is the culminating piece of the exercises. In the Unitive Way, we reflect on the inescapable reality of eternal life and Heaven. As life progresses, we all move towards eternity.

This is a fact about Christian life. We all have to live with the conviction that life has to be lived fully and faithfully in Christ. For Christians who love Mary and her Son Jesus, eternity is associated with Heaven. We shall attain salvation if we live our lives by imitating Mary and following in the footsteps of Jesus in our daily life. We will be with Mary both here and hereafter. **(79)**

Giraud suggests reflection on three things Mary tried to instill in our minds and hearts at her apparition.

His first point: she kept crying as she "climbed the knoll" until she ascended into Heaven. She wants us to persevere in *doing penance in our daily lives.*

> That is the best way to combat sins as humanly as possible. Even habitual sins can be and will have to be eradicated from our lives through penance that purifies our memory and prevents our imagination from the stain of sins. Penance paves the way to God's grace, which in turn strengthens us, to persevere in the practice of penance. God's grace helps us to be sincerely sorrowful for our sins.

> Consequently, our focus is directed towards the forgiving and reconciling love of God rather than the fear of sins and judgement. Our conscience becomes defensive against the onslaught of sins and thus purer. Our faithfulness to God's love becomes unshakable. Our trust in God's love can never be altered. Neither shall we lose our "fever" to avoid sins.

> Eventually, "our spiritual life [is] entirely infused with light, strength and charity" to the extent that we will not miss our goal, which is Heaven. **(80)**

His second point: To continue to reflect on what the apparition taught us, Giraud presents a second point. He said that Mary's feet were suspended in the air all the while she proceeded to the spot from which she ascended into Heaven. Although her feet touched the grass at times, the blades of grass never bent. This means, Giraud argues, that *Mary reminds us of our earthly sojourn.* And that *our Christian lives have to be untouched by the stains of worldly things.*

> We have to keep our hearts pure by detaching ourselves from secular things that taint our sanctity. We are pilgrims of the earth en route to Heaven. Our hearts naturally and truly yearn for the

**Painting of pilgrims filling the sight of
the Apparition on the Holy Mountain**

things of Heaven. This capacity of ours for transcendent realities is a gift from God. For these reasons, everything in this earthly life is secondary in comparison to anything in eternity.

Therefore, Mary teaches us to live in the freedom of God's love, that is, totally free from sins, until we all are united with her in the eternal home. **(81)**

Numbers 10 and 13 of the La Salette *Rule of Life* specifically require those who live La Salette spirituality, especially those who take evangelical vow of poverty, take to heart and live out a life worthy of freedom. It asks all to free themselves from the enslavement of immoderate use of worldly things. Here misuse and abuse of things are prohibited.

Everything that is essentially excessive has to be allotted and used for the welfare of the needy. Everyone is called to live a simple and modest lifestyle. This is in fact manifested by Mary herself during her apparition. Everything has to be used for the good of everyone in the community and in society as Jesus mandates it.

His third point: Giraud recounts a third point on the experience of the two children. The children claimed their willingness to go with Mary to Heaven right away even after a transitory encounter with her.

Mary shows us at La Salette the beauty and joy of being in the grace of God. She teaches us that "intimate, deep, loving and continual union is unfailing means to salvation."

> We are invited to live with her and for God by living in love, grace and charity in our relationship with others by praying regularly and faithfully. With the help of God's grace, we see and undergo sufferings through the eyes of faith. We come to understand that suffering is meant for the forgiveness of our sins and reconciliation with God whose glory we will definitely share someday.

> She teaches us to gaze at things with love and concern as well as have undying apostolic zeal. The zeal we have must include our humility, sincerity, genuineness, and generosity both to God and to all we meet every day. **(82)**

Mary invites us, Giraud contends, to consecrate our lives to [her protection] so that she will guide us in this unitive stage. Our lives have to cease to be the cause of her sorrow. Our sins should never make her tears shed again. We unite ourselves with her in her sorrow for the sins of those who go knowingly and unknowingly astray from God. Suffering for her and with her gives meaning in our lives for we are united with Christ Crucified and herself who cried at La Salette.

We have the responsibility to spread her message of God's love and concern for all. Specifically, the rejects of society must know that Jesus and Mary suffer with them and will bring them home to Heaven someday. Ministers of forgiveness and reconciliation have to work hard with unfailing zeal until all are united with Mary and Jesus in Heaven. **(83)** How to do it in daily chores/events might be the question.

Schlewer provides *steps to concretely exercise* the ministry of forgiveness and reconciliation.

- First, ministers have to renounce and denounce individualistic mentality and attitude to "take personal responsibility, in one way or another, for the devastating conflicts in our world."

• Second, they have to live as believers who help reshape the world according to God's design, as they have done it for past generations.

• Third, they have to "reveal and manifest this twofold dimension of human existence," i.e., taking personal responsibility for miseries in the world and living out one's faith in God to impact the world around them, in their daily lives. **(84)**

The Unitive Way helps us to live in God's grace after the example of the Blessed Mother. The Unitive Way also helps us to put heaven into perspective in our daily lives and to imitate the Blessed Mother who was united with Christ her Son since the day of singing her Magnificat (Luke 1:46-55). She did it in her ordinary daily life.

Pope Benedict XVI greets the people

Pope Benedict XVI in his encyclical, *Deus Caritas Est*, said that Mary is in perfect communion with God's Word (Luke 1:26-38) to the extent that everything she says and does reflects God's Word. Her words and God's Word become one in her life. Her whole life is "attuned to" God's life. That made her to be the worthy Mother of Jesus. Her whole life also reflects Jesus' simplicity, humility, love and fidelity to the will of the Father.

In the merits of her Son, Jesus, she did everything she had to do as a sign of her union with God both here and hereafter. She is the role model for all Christians as she was for the Apostles on the day of Pentecost and afterwards. **(85)**

Conclusion...

We discussed Giraud's three ways of Christian spirituality in the light of the La Salette message. We also discussed the La Salette way of life that reflects the message of Our Lady of La Salette, particularly the three pillars of La Salette Spirituality. We see the importance of praying, doing penance and having undying apostolic zeal. Each way is built upon and geared towards each other for without one the other can't be done or has no meaning. We see that every spiritual exercise Giraud espouses has God at the center. Each has Jesus as the visible sign of God's forgiveness and reconciliation. Each way points out the invitation, encouragement, warning and commissioning of Mary to all God's people.

More specifically, we discussed Sylvain-Marie Giraud's La Salette Spiritual Exercises of Christian Spirituality that emphasize:

> 1) **the Purgative Way** in La Salette spirituality that requires doing penance daily in communion with Jesus and the Blessed Mother for the sins of others and our own as the Blessed Mother told the two visionaries by the name of Maximin and Melanie during her apparition at La Salette,

> 2) **the Illuminative Way** in La Salette spirituality means living in the light of Christ that shines forth from the Crucifix worn by the Blessed Mother during her apparition at La Salette as described by the visionaries by the name of Maximin and Melanie,

> 3) **the Unitive Way** in La Salette spirituality is the way and the goal of Christian life as it is conveyed in the message and ascension of the Blessed Mother during her apparition at La Salette.

We also see the menace of sin that distances us from God, others and ourselves. What is striking is God's loving concern for His people. The indubitable reality of God's forgiving and reconciling love accompanies His people. God knows what His people have to go through daily.

Although everything they endure in life is because of the sins of others or those of their own, God sent Mary to remind them of sin, judgement, and their need to return to Him. Catholic parents must avail themselves of God's forgiveness and reconciliation so that they may forgive and reconcile with themselves, others and God.

Catholic parents, who are ministers of forgiveness and reconciliation, are called to make this message known to all who are on the Christian journey in their respective families. Catholic parents can practice the La Salette Spiritual Exercises as a way of life after the example of the Blessed Virgin Mary who appeared at La Salette, France on September 19, 1846. Catholic parents can be involved in the ministry of forgiveness and reconciliation in their personal and familial life until they reach Heaven where Mary and Jesus await them.

Mass for Reestablishment of La Salette Mission in Myanmar in 2005

For your reflection:

Scripture: Luke 2: 48-52 (*How parenting even for the Holy Family was a challenge*)

> ...When his parents saw Jesus in the Temple, they were astonished, and his mother said to him, "Son, why have you done this to us? Your father and I have been looking for you with great anxiety." And he said to them, "Why were you looking for me? Did you not know that I must be in my Father's house?" But they did not understand what he said to them.
>
> He went down with them and came to Nazareth, and was obe-

dient to them; and his mother kept all these things in her heart. And Jesus advanced in wisdom and age and favor before God and man.

Reflection Questions:
• When have you seen little hopeful events within your family which have encouraged you to keep making efforts to love each of them?
• What has been most challenging in living within your family or parenting your children?
• What help do you need to pray for concerning your family?
• Other comments.....

Prayer:
Mary, Spouse of the Holy Spirit, we see in your own family at Nazareth the challenge of parenting your child. Strengthen us by your prayer that we may grow in wisdom and age and grace before God and our own family members. We ask this through your intercession and in the grace of your Son who lives with the Father and the Holy Spirit, God, for ever and ever. **Amen.**

La Salette Invocation:
Our Lady of La Salette, Reconciler of Sinners, pray without ceasing for us who have recourse to you.

Chapter Six:
Where Do We Go From Here?

**Pilgrims gather in prayer around
La Salette Ascension statue on the Holy Mountain**

What's next, now that we've been led through a full explanation of the practical family La Salette Spirituality? We truly believe that parents can become "leading-learners" as Thomas H. Groome in his book, *Sharing Faith*, puts it. Parents can "remain open to be led by" everyone they journey with "to greater holiness and wholeness in Christian living."

Everything parents say and do affects both others and themselves. Witnessing is a lifetime journey that challenges everyone involved to hone their gifts, talents and ways of communication in the ministry of sharing the faith," **(1)** especially forgiveness and reconciliation.

The U.S. Bishops rightly stated: "It is through the example of mothers and fathers, grandparents, siblings, and extended family members that one most concretely witnesses how to live a Christian life" **(2)** Thus, if parents live their faith, sharing the forgiveness of God in their homes, their children will naturally learn to forgive themselves and others.

Live the message and share it with others!

La Salette spirituality needs to be shared with and by ordinary people, especially with Catholic parents, just as Mary shared her message with the two young unsuspecting children. It can foster growth in Catholic parents' spiritual life as they first are able to experience and then to share forgiveness and reconciliation in their relationships with others by the grace of God.

The U.S. bishops state that "the commitment to living the Christian life provides an essential element of the culture of witness. To those seeking answers to the increasing secularization, individualism, and materialism of society, a Christian life provides a powerful witness to the Gospel" **(2) Committee on Evangelization** and Catechesis: United States Conference of Catholic Bishops, Disciples Called to Witness: The New Evangelization, 11-12).

Family-picnic on the Irawaddy River in Myanmar

As forgiveness and reconciliation are needed more and more due to the rise and influence of all the "isms" the bishops mention above, "reconciliation will be needed more, not less" in personal and familial situations. **(3)**

Catholic parents are called to share the message of forgiving and reconciling love of God offered by Jesus and reminded by the Blessed Virgin Mary at La Salette in France on September 19, 1846.

We are truly hopeful that this new synthesis of understanding our biblical call from St. Paul to be reconcilers (2 Corinthians 5:18), linked together with Mary's mandate at La Salette and its own special spirituality will help Catholic parents become a more vital part of the ministry of forgiveness and reconciliation to all Mary's people, beginning with their own families.

Endnotes

(1) Pope St. John Paul II in his encyclical letter, *Centisimus Annus*, 39.

(2) Congregation for the Doctrine of Faith, *The Message of Fatima*, Fatima, 13 May 2000.

(3) Marcel Schlewer, M.S., *All My People: Why She Spoke-Why She Wept at La Salette*, 2-4.

(4) Address of The Holy Father John Paul II to The Missionaries of Our Lady of La Salette, Thursday, 4 May 2000.

General Introduction...pg.

(1) The La Salette *Rule of Life*, pgs. 27-28.

(2) Giraud, *Editions de la Revue des Alpes*, Grenoble, le 15 de Février, 1945.

Settings the Scene – A Glossary of Terms...pg

(1) Normand Theroux, *The Face of the Reconciler: Sharing the La Salette Charism of Reconciliation*, 14, 25.

(2) Vincent Taylor, *Forgiveness and Reconciliation: A Study in New Testament Theology*, 4)

(3) *Ibidem*, 28.

(4) Doris Donnelly, *Putting Forgiveness into Practice*, 1.

(5) Robert Schreiter, *The Ministry of Reconciliation: Spirituality & Strategies*, 55, 57, 58).

(6) Normand Theroux, *The Face of the Reconciler: Sharing the La Salette Charism of Reconciliation*, 5).

(7) Giraud, 165.

(8) Giraud, 119.

(9) Schreiter, *The Ministry of Reconciliation: Spirituality & Strategies*, 14.

(10) Schreiter, *The Ministry of Reconciliation: Spirituality & Strategies*, 12, 65.

(11) Giraud, *The Book of the Spiritual Exercises of Our Lady of La Salette*, 66.

(12) Monica Hellwig, *Sign of Reconciliation and Conversion: The Sacrament of Penance for Our Times*, 6.

Part One:
Forgiveness and Reconciliation
in the Early Church

Chapter One:
Forgiveness and Reconciliation in the Early Church

(1) James Dallen, *The Reconciling Community: The Rite of Penance*, 18-19.

(2) *Ibidem*, 21.

(3) *Ibidem*, 22-24.

(4) Frans Jozef van Beek, *"Praise and Thanksgiving in Non-eucharistic Communion Services,"* 424.

(5) Hellwig, *Sign of Reconciliation and Conversion: The Sacrament of Penance for Our Times*, 30-31.

(6) Marty Slaughter, "Sublime Mercy," 437-450.

Chapter Two:
Theological Foundations of Forgiveness and Reconciliation

(1) Constitution on the Sacred Liturgy, *Sacrosanctum Concilium*, 5.

(2) *Lumen Gentium*, 11.

(3) *Ibidem*, 31.

(4) *Gaudium et Spes*, 1-8, 12-13.

(5) *Ibidem*, 13)

(6) International Theological Commission, *Memory and Reconciliation: The Church and the Faults of the Past*, 3, 3.1, 3.3.

(7) *Ibidem*, 1.

(8) *Ibidem*, 1.3, 1.4)

(9) Pope St. John Paul II, *Reconciliatio et Paenitentia*, 5, 6.

(10) *Ibidem*, 4.

(11) Pope St. John Paul II, *Dives in Misericordia*, 5, 6.

(12) *Reconciliatio et Paenitentia*, 4, 5, 7.

(13) *Ibidem*, 8.

(14) *Ibidem*.

(15) Pope Francis, *Misericordiae Vultus*, 9.

(16) Pope Francis, *Amoris Laetitia*, 313-317.

(17) *Ibidem*, 105-106).

(18) *Ibidem*, 107.

(19) *Ibidem*, 274-279.

(20) The Catholic Family in Asia: *Domestic Church of the Poor on a Mission of Mercy*, 3-17, 21-22.

(21) *Ibidem*, 28.

(22) *Ibidem*, 52.

(23) *Ad Gentes*, 10, 11.

(24) *Ibidem*, 12.

(25) *Ibidem*, 24).

Chapter Three:

The Scriptural Viewpoint of

Forgiveness and Reconciliation

within Relationships

(1) Pope Benedict XVI, Verbum Domini, 8).

(2) Vincent Taylor, 24-27, 32.

(3) J. Edward Owens, "Numbers 13:1-14:45" in *The Paulist Biblical Commentary*, 124, 134; see Exodus 34:6-7, Nehemiah 9:17, Ps. 103: 8-13, and Jonah 4:2.

(4) Frederick L. Moriarty, "Numbers 14:1-45" in *The Jerome Biblical Commentary*, 91.

(5) Deidre Dempsey, "Hosea 2:14-23" in *The Paulist Biblical Commentary*, 803.

(6) Dennis McCarthy, "Hosea 2:14-23" in *The Jerome Biblical Commentary*, 257; see also Hosea 2:18-25.

(7) *Ibidem*, 257.

(8) Bruce Vawter, "The Johannine Epistles: John 15:1-17" in *The Jerome Biblical Commentary*, 454.

(9) Sandra Schneiders, "*The Lamb of God and the Forgiveness of Sin (s) in the Fourth Gospel*," 2-5.

(10) *Ibidem*, 7-9.

(11) *Ibidem.*

(12) Joseph A. Fitzmyer, "The Letter to the Romans" in *The Jerome Biblical Commentary*, 305-306.

(13) Antonio Pitta, "Second Corinthians: 2 Corinthians 5:16-20" in *The Paulist Biblical Commentary*, 1361.

(14) John J. O'Rourke, "The Second Letter to the Corinthians: 2 Corinthians 5:16-21" in *The Jerome Biblical Commentary*, 281)

(15) Joseph Plevnik, "The Understanding of God at the Basis of Pauline Theology," 556-557,559, 561, 565, 567.

(16) Mark Gignilliat, "A Servant Follower of the Servant: Paul's Eschatological Reading of Isaiah 40-66 in 2 Corinthians 5:14-6:10," 110-111, 115-122.

(17) Rudolf Bultmann, *Theology of the New Testament*, 2 Volumes, 285-287.

(18) Vincent Taylor, *Forgiveness and Reconciliation: A Study in New Testament Theology*, 21-23.

(19) Antonio Pitta, "Second Corinthians" in *The Paulist Biblical Commentary*, 1361-1362.

(20) Pheme Perkins, *Reading the New Testament*, 186, 188.

(21) Carroll Stuhlmueller, "The Gospel According to Luke: Luke 15:11-32" in *The Jerome Biblical Commentary*, 148-149.

(22) Gerald O'Collins, *Jesus: A Portrait*, 119-120)

(23) Vincent Taylor, 266-269.

(24) Vincent Taylor, 270-275).

Chapter Four:

Various Scholars' Approaches to Forgiveness and Reconciliation

(1) Sandra Schneiders, her lecture, *The Spirit in the New Millennium*, 27.

(2) *Ibidem*, 28-33.

(3) Sandra Schneiders, "*The Lamb of God and the Forgiveness of Sin (s) in the Fourth Gospel*," 13-15.

(4) *Ibidem*, 17.

(5) *Ibidem*, 21-23.

(6) *Ibidem*, 23- 24)

(7) Michael Hurley, *The Ecumenical Methodology of Forgiveness*, 55-56.

(8) *Ibidem*, 360-368.

(9) Raymond G. Helmick and Rodney L. Petersen, "*Forgiveness and Reconciliation: Religion, Public Policy and Conflict Transformation*," 13, 14-15.

(10) Doris Donnelly, *Putting Forgiveness into Practice*, 19.

(11) *Ibidem*, 20.

(12) Louis Bouyer, *Dictionary of Theology*, 294-295.

(13) Doris Donnelly, 21.

(14) *Ibidem*, 24.

(15) Robert Schreiter, *The Ministry of Reconciliation: Spirituality and Strategies*, 55-56.

(16) *Ibidem*, 14,16.

(17) *Ibidem*, 58.

(18) Robert Schreiter, in his talk, "*The Ministry of Forgiveness in a Prax-*

is of Reconciliation" at the International Seminar on Reconciliation," 3.

(19) William Nordenbrock, in his talk, "*Ministry of Reconciliation: Methods Rooted in Spirituality*," 2.

(20) Robert Schreiter, in his article, "*Justice and Reconciliatio*," 3.

(21) Robert Schreiter, *The Ministry of Forgiveness and Reconciliation: Spirituality and Strategies*, 56-57.

(22) *Ibidem*, 56-57.

(23) One's way of life can completely change due to forgiveness and reconciliation. It can effect change in others' lives, too. Schreiter argues that reconciliation is a way of life because it pertains more to spiritual realities.

(24) Robert Schreiter, *The Ministry of Reconciliation: Spirituality and Strategies*, 16; and Schreiter, Reconciliation: Mission and Ministry in a Changing Social Order, 42-43.

(25) Marian Maskulak, in her article, "*A Spirituality of Reconciliation: Lessons from Rwanda*," 535, 539.

(26) William Nordenbrock, "*Ministry of Reconciliation: Methods Rooted in Spirituality*," 3.

(27) Monica Hellwig, *Sign of Reconciliation and Conversion: The Sacrament of Penance for Our Time*, 13-15.

(28) *Ibidem*, 16-17.

(29) *Ibidem*, 18-21.

(30) *Ibidem*, 22-23.

(31) *Ibidem*, 24-26.

(32) Brian P. Flanagan, in his article, "*Reconciliation and the Church: A Response to Bruce Morrill*," 629-634.

(33) see Benjamin Brown, in his article, "*Raymond Schwager on the*

Dramatic Justice and Mercy of God," 214-220.

(34) Normand Theroux, M.S., *The Face of the Reconciler*, 2.

(35) *Ibidem*, 5.

(36) *Ibidem*, 16-40.

(37) *Ibidem*, 62-64.

Part Two:
Principles for Living Out
Christian Forgiveness and Reconciliation...

Chapter Five:
Giraud's Spiritual Exercises as
Rooted in the La Salette Message

(1) Emile A. Ladouceur, M.S., *The Vision of La Salette: The Children Speak*, 14-15.

(2) The La Salette *Rule of Life*, Prologue, pg 21.

Our La Salette Rule states in the Prologue that Philibert de Bruil-lard, Bishop of Grenoble, in a pastoral letter, dated May 1, 1852 the Bishop of Grenoble announced the construction of a Shrine on the mountain of the apparition, and went on to add,

> *"However important the erection of a shrine maybe, there was something still more important, namely the ministers of religion destined to look after it, to receive the pious pilgrims, to preach the word of God to them, to exercise toward them the ministry of reconciliation, to administer the Holy Sacrament of the altar, and to be, to all, the faithful dispensers of the mysteries of God and the spiritual treasures of the Church."*

He continued:

> "These priests shall be called the Missionaries of Our Lady of La Salette; their institution and existence shall be, like the shrine itself, and eternal monuments, a perpetual remembrance, of Mary's merciful apparition."

(3) La Salette *Rule of Life*, 27, Constitutions, #1, #2.

Our La Salette *Rule of Life* also states:

> 1) Among the people of God we, the Missionaries of Our Lady of La Salette, form a religious apostolic Congregation dedicated to the ministry of reconciliation.

> 2) Our Congregation is made up of priests and brothers bound together by the same religious vocation. We are defined by the Holy See as a clerical religious institute of Pontifical right.

(4) The La Salette *Rule of Life*, Constitutions, #23.

> 23) Drawing our inspiration from the message of Our Lady of La Salette, we dedicate ourselves to:

> • the reconciliation of sinners and the liberation of all people through submission to the will of the Father;
> • the awakening and deepening of faith among the People of God so that every human reality may be illumined by the light of the Gospel;
> • the proclamation of the Good News where it is not yet known;
> • the promotion of mutual understanding among religions and their coming together in charity and truth;
> • the struggle against those evils which now compromise the salvific plan of God and the dignity of the human person.

In these various apostolic commitments we stress the incomparable role Mary fulfilled in salvation history and which is still hers in the life of the Church.

(5) Sylvain-Marie Giraud, M.S., *Le Livre des Exercices Spirituels de Notre-Dame de La Salette*, Editions de la Revue des Alpes. Grenoble: 1946).

(6) Sylvain-Marie Giraud, M.S., *The Book of the Spiritual Exercises of Our Lady of La Salette*, introduction, notes and translation by Donald Paradis, M.S., Grassroots Publishing, Enfield, New Hampshire, 2005.

(7) Jon Sobrino, *Christology at the Crossroads*, 50-51.

(8) *Ibidem*, 52-60.

(9) Mitch and Kathy Finley, *Building Christian Familie,s* 93-105.

(10) Sylvain-Marie Giraud, M.S., *The Spiritual Exercises of Our Lady of La Salette*, 18-19.

(11) Normand Theroux, M.S., *The Face of the Reconciler: Sharing the La Salette Charism of Reconciliation*, 8-13.

(12) *Ibidem*, 14.

(13) David E. Rosage, *Reconciliation: The Sacramental Path to Peace*, 16-17.

(14) J. N. D. Kelly, *Early Christian Doctrines*, 362-364.

(15) Sylvain-Marie Giraud, M.S., *The Spiritual Exercises of Our Lady of La Salette*, 24-26.

(16) Normand Theroux, *The Face of the Reconciler*, 15-20.

(17) David E. Rosage, 19-21.

(18) The La. Salette *Rule of Life*, 6:

> 6) We emphasize the profoundly evangelical values of prayer, penance and zeal contained in the message of Our Lady of La Salette which calls us to conversion. We strive to live them ourselves so that, by the witness of our lives as well as by our words, hearts may be opened to the Good News which it is our mission to

make known to all.

(19) Sylvain-Marie Giraud, *The Spiritual Exercises of Our Lady of La Salette*, 119-121.

(20) Jon Sobrino, *Christology at the Crossroads*, 150-151.

(21) *Ibidem*, 152-155.

(22) Agnes Cunningham, *Prayer: Personal and Liturgical*, 17-19.

(23) *Ibidem*, 47-48.

(24) Pope Benedict XVI, *Spe Salvi*, 33-34)

(25) Christopher Wells, "*Pope Francis Announces Extraordinary Urbi et Orbi Blessing*," March 22, 2020.

(26) Giraud, 122-124.

(27) Agnes Cunningham, *Prayer: Personal and Liturgical*, 45-58.

(28) Ralph Martin, *The Fulfillment of All Desire*, 125-128.

(29) Agnes Cunningham, *Prayer: Personal and Liturgical*, 58-63).

(30) Brendan Byrne, "Matthew 6:9-15" in *The Paulist Biblical Commentary*, 922-923.

(31) Agnes Cunningham, *Prayer: Personal and Liturgical*, 63-65.

(32) see Giraud, 119-121.

Bibliography

La Salette Matha Province members meet in India

Primary Sources:

Benedict XVI Pope. Encyclical Letter, *Deus Caritas Est* (*On Christian Love*). December 25, 2005.

Benedict XVI Pope. Encyclical Letter, *Spe Salvi* (*On Christian Hope*). November 30, 2007.

Benedict XVI Pope. Post-Synodal Apostolic Exhortation, *Verbum Domini* (*On the Word of God*). September 30, 2010.

Committee on Evangelization and Catechesis: The United States Conference of Catholic Bishops. *Disciples Called to Witness: The New Evangelization* (Washington, DC: United States Conference of Catholic Bishops, 2012).

Federation of Asian Bishops Conference. *The Catholic Family in Asia: Domestic Church of the Poor on a Mission of Mercy*. FABC Papers No. 151 (28 November - 4 December 2016).

Francis, Pope. Bull of Indiction, *Misericordiae Vultus (The Extraordinary Jubilee of Mercy)*. April 11, 2015.

Francis, Pope. Apostolic Letter, *Misericordia et Misera (The Conclusion of the Extraordinary Jubilee of Mercy)*. November 20, 2016. Holy See.\.

International Theological Commission. *Memory and Reconciliation: The Church and the Faults of the Past* (December 1999). Holy See.

John Paul II. Encyclical Letter, *Centesimus Annus*. May 1, 1991. Holy See.

John Paul II. Post-Synodal Apostolic Exhortation, *Reconciliatio et Paenitentia*. December 2, 1984.

John Paul II, Apostolic Letter, *Novo Millennio Inuente (The Close of the Great Jubilee Year 2000)*. Jan. 6, 2001.

John Paul II. *"Address of the Holy Father John Paul II to the Missionaries of our Lady of La Salette,"* 29th General Chapter (4 May 2000), 1-2.

John Paul II. Encyclical Letter, *Dives in Misericordia (Rich in Mercy)*, November 30, 1980.

La Salette Congregation, *Rule of Life of the Missionaries of Our Lady of La Salette*. Tipografia Poliglotta Della Pontificia Universita Gregoriana: Roma, 2 Februarii, 1987.

The Catechism of the Catholic Church (Libreria Editrice Vaticana, 1993).

Vatican II. Dogmatic Constitution, *Dei Verbum (On Divine Revelation)*, November 18, 1965).

Vatican II. *"Dogmatic Constitution, Lumen Gentium (On the Church),* 21 November, 1964," in Vatican Council II: The Conciliar and Post Conciliar Documents, edited by Austin Flannery (Northport, NY: Costello Publishing Company, 1996).

Vatican II. Pastoral Constitution, *Gaudium et Spes (Church in the Modern World)*, December 7, 1965.

Secondary Sources:

Appleby, R. Scott. "Toward a Theology and Praxis of Reconciliation." *Journal of Ecumenical Studies*, 39, no. 1-2 (2002): 132.

Bellitto, Christopher M. "Teaching the Church's Mistakes: Historical Hermeneutics in Memory and Reconciliation: The Church and the Faults of the Past." *Horizons* 32, no. 1 (2005): 123-135..

Bibliotheca Ephemeridum Theologicarum Lovaniensium, *The Household of God and Local Households; Revisiting the Domestic Church*, edited by Thomas Knieps- Port Le Roi, Gerard Mannion and Peter De Mey. Walpole, Massachusetts, 2013.

Boers, Hendrikus. "2 Corinthians 5:14-6:2: A Fragment of Pauline Christology." *The Catholic Biblical Quarterly*, 64, no. 3 (July 2002): 527-547.

Bouyer, Louis. *Dictionary of Theology*, translated by Charles Underhill Quinn. Belgium: Tournai, Desclee Co., Inc., 1965.

Brink, Laurie. "From Wrongdoer to New Creation: Reconciliation in 2 Corinthians." *Interpretation: A Journal of Bible and Theology*, 71, no. 3 (2017): 298-309.

Brown, Benjamin. "Raymund Schwager on the Dramatic Justice and Mercy of God." *International Journal of Systematic Theology*, 17, no. 2 (2015): 212-228. doi:10.1111/ijst.12098.

Brown, Raymond E., Joseph Fitzmyer, and Roland Murphy. *The Jerome Biblical Commentary*. Englewood Cliffs, New Jersey: Prentice-Hall, Inc., 1968)

Bultmann, Rudolf. *Theology of the New Testament*, 2 Volumes, translated by Kendrick Grobel. Waco, TX: Baylor University Press, 2007.

Coffey, D. "*The Future of the Sacrament of Penance*." Theological Studies, [s.1] 69, n.2 (2008): 480-481

Chiu, Jose Enrique Aguilar, Richard J. Clifford, Carol J. Dempsey, Eileen M. Schuller, Thomas D. Stegman and Ronald D. Witherup. *The Paulist Biblical Commentary*. Mahwah, NJ: Paulist Press, 2018.

Cunningham, Agnes. *Prayer: Personal and Liturgical, (Message of the Fathers of the Church)*, edited by Thomas Halton and Michael Glazier (Wilmington, Delaware, 1985).

Dallen, James. *The Reconciling Community: The Rite of Penance (Studies in the Reformed Rites of The Catholic Church, Volume III)*. Pueblo Publishing, NY, 1986.

Doherty, William. *A Brief History of the La Salette Mission in Burma*. Attleborro, MA: La Salette Communication Center Publications, 2012.

Donnelly, Doris. *Putting Forgiveness into Practice*. Allen, TX: Argus Communications, 1982.

Duchame, Jamie. "World Health Organization Declares COVID-19 a 'Pandemic.' Here is What It Means." *TIME*. March 11, 2020.

Emma and Anderson. "Changing Devotional Paradigms and their Impact upon Nineteenth-Century Marian Apparitions: The Case of La Salette." in *Union Seminary Quarterly Review* 52, nos. 3-4 (1998): 85-122.

Falconer, Alan. "Mercy as the Essence of the Gospel: Key Themes in Walter Kasper and in the Ministry of Pope Francis." *International Journal for the Study of the Christian Church* 15, no. 3 (2015): 244-253.

Farrell, Marie. "The Mercy of the Lord Endures Forever." in *Compass* 49, no. 4 (2015): 6.

Flanagan, Brian P. "Reconciliation and the Church: A Response to Bruce Morrill." *Theological Studies* 75, no. 3 (2014): 624-634.

Fink, Peter E. "Investigating the Sacrament of Penance: An Experiment in Sacramental Theology." *Worship* [s.l] 54, no. 3 (1980): 206-220.

Gallagher, Raphael. "Law Or Mercy? The Pastoral Nature of Moral

Theology." in *The Furrow* 51, no. 3 (2000): 139-147.

Gignilliat, Mark. "A Servant Follower of the Servant: Paul's Eschatological Reading of Isaiah 40-66 in 2 Corinthians 5:14-6:10." *Horizons in Biblical Theology* 26, no. 1 (2004): 98-124.

Giraud, Sylvain-Marie, M.S., *The Book of the Spiritual Exercises of Our Lady of La Salette*, translated by Donald Paradis. Enfield, New Hampshire: Grassroots Publishing International, 2005.

Hellwig, Monica K., *Sign of Reconciliation and Conversion: The Sacrament of Penance for Our Times*. Wilmington, Delaware: Michael Glazier, Inc., Revised Edition, 1984.

Hurley, Michael. "The Ecumenical Methodology of Forgiveness." *Irish Theological Quarterly* 68, no. 4 (Sage Publications, Dec. 2003):357–377.

Jaouen, Jean, M.S., *A Grace Called La Salette: A Story for the World*, translated by Normand Theroux. Enfield, New Hampshire: Grassroots Publishing International, 1991.

Jordan, Elizabeth. "Reconciling Women: A Feminist Reading of the History of Confession in the Roman Catholic Tradition." *Australian Feminist Studies* 14, no. 30 (1999): 303-313.

Keenan, James F. "Receiving Amoris Laetitia." *Theological Studies* 78, no. 1 (2017): 193-212.

Kelly, Anthony J. "The Body of Christ: Amen!: The Expanding Incarnation." *Theological Studies* 71, no. 4 (2010): 792-816.

Kelly, Gerard. "The Justice and Mercy of God." *The Australasian Catholic Record* 3, no. 2 (2016): 198-208.

Kelly, J. N. D. *Early Christian Doctrines*. Rev. ed. New York, New York: HarperCollins Publishers, 1978.

Lam, Joseph. "Mercy, Happiness and Human Growth in the Teaching of Pope Francis." *The Australasian Catholic Record* 3, no. 4 (2016): 435-446.

MacDonald, Nathan. "Listening to Abraham-Listening to Yhwh: Divine Justice and Mercy in Genesis 18:16-33." *The Catholic Biblical Quarterly* 66, no. 1 (01, 2004): 25-43.

Martin, Ralph. *The Fulfillment of All Desire: A Guidebook for the Journey to God Based on the Wisdom of the Saints.* Steubenville, Ohio: Emmaus Road Publishing, 2006.

Maskulak, Marian. "A Spirituality of Reconciliation: Lessons from Rwanda." *New Blackfriars* 98, no. 1077 (2017): 521-538.

Morrill, Bruce T. "Sign of Reconciliation and Conversion? Differing Views of Power—Ecclesial, Sacramental, Anthropological—among Hierarchy and Laity." *Theological Studies* 75, no. 3 (2014): 585-612.

Nordenbrock, William. "Ministry of Reconciliation: Methods Rooted in Spirituality." *Missionaries of La Salette Keynote.* Orlando, Florida. October 25, 2010.

O'Collins, Gerald. *Jesus: A Portrait.* Maryknoll, New York: Orbis Books, 2008.

Pandarakalam, James Paul. "Understanding the La Salette Apparition." *The Journal for Spiritual and Consciousness Studies* 38, no. 1 (2015): 25-35.

Paradis, Donald, M.S., *The Missionaries of La Salette: From France to America.* Attleboro, Massachusetts: La Salette Publications, 1992.

Perkins, Pheme *Reading the New Testament*, 2nd Edition. Paulist Press, New York, 1988.

Plevnik, Joseph. "The Understanding of God at the Basis of Pauline Theology." *The Catholic Biblical Quarterly* 65, no. 4 (10, 2003): 554-567.

Rosage, David E. *Reconciliation: The Sacramental Path to Peace.* Locust Valley, New York: Living Flame Press, 1984.

Rush, Ormond. "Ecclesial Conversion after Vatican II: Renewing 'the Face of the Church" to the Reflect the Genuine Face of God". *Theolog-*

ical Studies 74, no. 4 (2013): 785-803.

Schlewer, Marcel, M.S., *All My People: Why She Spoke, Why She Wept at La Salette*. Enfield, New Hampshire: Grassroots Publishing International, 1998.

Scholl, Edith. "Mercy within Mercy: Misericordia and Miseria." *Cistercian Studies Quarterly* 42, no. 1 (2007): 63.

Schneiders, Sandra Marie. "Whose Sins You Shall Forgive…. The Holy Spirit and the Forgiveness of Sin (s) in the Fourth Gospel." (2009).

Schneiders, Sandra M. "The Lamb of God and the Forgiveness of Sin in the Fourth Gospel." *The Catholic Biblical Quarterly* 73, no. 1 (2011)

Schreiter, Robert J. "Justice and Reconciliation." *Justice, Peace and the Integrity of Creation Commission* (Union Superiors General and International Union of Superiors General, Rome) November 30, 2009.

Schreiter, Robert J. "Reconciliation and Healing as a Paradigm for Mission." *International Review of Mission* 94. no. 572 (January 2005): 75-84.

Schreiter, Robert J. "The Charism of Reconciliation and Its Practices." *Missionaries of La Salette Chapter Keynote*. Orlando, FL, October 26, 2009.

Schreiter, Robert J. "The Ministry of Forgiveness in a Praxis of Reconciliation." *International Seminar on Reconciliation* (Lima, 21 August, 2006).

Sobrino, Jon. *Christology at the Crossroads*, trans. John Drury. Orbis Books, Maryknoll, New York, 1978.

Slaughter, Marty. "Sublime Mercy." *Law, Culture and the Humanities* 6, no. 3 (2010): 436-454.

Spitzer, Robert. *Five Pillars of the Spiritual Life: A Practical Guide to Prayer for Active People*. San Francisco, California: Ignatius Press, 2008.

Theroux, Normand, M.S., *Food for the Journey: The Biblical Roots of the La Salette Message, Volume One*. Hartford, Connecticut: Missionaries of La Salette Corporation, Maple Avenue, September 19, 2017.

Theroux, Normand., M.S., *Our La Salette Mission: To Reconcile Her People With Her Son*, edited by Ron Gagne. Hartford, Connecticut: Missionaries of La Salette Corporation, Maple Avenue, September 19, 2017.

Theroux, Normand, M.S., *The Face of the Reconciler: Sharing the La Salette Charism of Reconciliation*. Attleboro, Massachusetts: La Salette Communications Center Publications, 2014.

The United States Conference of Catholic Bishops. "Prayers of the Rosary."

Valiente, O. Ernesto. "From Conflict to Reconciliation: Discipleship in the Theology of Jon Sobrino." *Theological Studies* 74, no. 3 (2013): 655-682.

Wells, Christopher. "Pope Francis Announces Extraordinary *Urbi et Orbi* Blessing," the Holy See, March 22, 2020.

World Health Organization. "The Report of the WHO-China Joint Mission for Coronavirus Disease 2019 (COVID-19)."

Methodology:

Downey, Michael. *Understanding Christian Spirituality*. Mawah: N.J, Paulist Press, 1997.

Knowles, Malcolm S., Elwood F. Holton III, and Richard A. Swanson. *The Adult Learner*. New York: Routlefge, 2015.

Groome, Thomas H. Sharing Faith: *A Comprehensive Approach to Religious Education and Pastoral Ministry*. Oregon, Eugene: Wipf and Stock Publishers, 1998.

Further Recommended Reading:

Leslie, Gillian. "Julian of Norwich and the Theology of Forgiveness. *The Living Pulpit* [s.1.], v. 3, n. 2, 26-27, 1994.

Maguire, Daniel C. "Redefining the Ministry of Reconciliation." *National Catholic Reporter* (1999).

McConville, J. Gordon. "Forgiveness as Private and Public Act: A Reading of the Biblical Joseph Narrative." *The Catholic Biblical Quarterly*, [s. 1.], v.75, n. 4, 635-648, 2013.

Tutu, Desmond Mpilo. *No Future Without Forgiveness.* New York: Image, Doubleday, 1999.

La Salette Bishop Donald Pelletier gathers the children after Mass in Ambodimanga, Madagascar

Made in the USA
Columbia, SC
18 January 2022

54396291R00083